A Williamson  Little Hands® Book

Around-the-World
Art & Activities

Visiting the 7 continents through craft fun

by Judy Press

Illustrations by Betsy Day

WILLIAMSON PUBLISHING  CHARLOTTE, VERMONT

Library of Congress Cataloging-in-Publication Data

Press, Judy, 1944-
   Around-the-world art & activities : visiting the 7 continents through craft fun / Judy Press.
     p. cm. -- (A Williamson Little Hands book)
   Includes index.
   ISBN 1-885593-45-7 (pbk.)
   1. Activity programs in education--Juvenile literature. 2. Handicraft--Study and teaching--Juvenile literature. 3. Multicultural education--Activity programs--Juvenile literature. I. Title. II. Series.

LB1027.25 .P74 2000
372.5'044--dc21

00-60030

Little Hands® series editor: **Susan Williamson**
Interior Design: **Nancy-jo Funaro**
Illustrations: **Betsy Day**
Cover design: **Trezzo-Braren Studio**
Printing: **Capital City Press**

Williamson Publishing Co.
P.O. Box 185
Charlotte, VT 05445
(800) 234-8791

Dedication

To my children

The journey of a thousand miles begins with a single step.
— LAO-TZU

Acknowledgments

I wish to thank the following people for their support and encouragement in the writing of this book: The Mt. Lebanon Public Library; the Carnegie Library of Pittsburgh; Carol Baicker McKee and Andrea Perry; and my husband, Allan, who knows the way without having to ask for directions.

This book would not have been possible without the talent and dedication of the following people at Williamson Publishing: Susan and Jack Williamson, Dana Pierson, Emily Stetson, June Roelle, Vicky Congdon, Jean Silveira, and Merietta McKenzie. A special thanks to designer Nancy-jo Funaro, illustrator Betsy Day, and Ken Braren and Loretta Trezzo at Trezzo-Braren Studio for their creative talents.

Contents

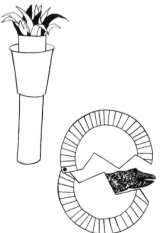

CONTINUED...

A Message to Grown-Ups

On this trip around the world, we'll stop on all seven continents and cross four oceans on an imaginative adventure that will enable children to build a wider view of the world. Our goal is to open kids' eyes to the wonder  of the world by introducing them to continents rather than countries (although we do provide site details).

Every journey starts with a travel plan. Our overall plan is to follow the sunrise, but you can choose your own route.  You might want to begin at home, where kids feel most comfortable. Or you might want to go where you yourself have traveled, to familiar sites that you can describe. Wherever you begin, look at the map on pages 10–11. Trace the route from home to the selected destination. Gather all the supplies you'll need to complete the craft. Then, let the fun begin!

Although specific instructions are provided for each project, always allow the child to make choices and follow his or her own muse. Avoid holding up perfectly completed projects that will only intimidate the young crafter and stifle creativity. Encourage new ideas, fanciful designs, and individualized interpretations so that each piece of art reflects the creativity and mood of the child who made it.

Some of the projects are more challenging to make than others. The globe symbols next to each project will guide you: One globe is the least challenging, and three globes may require more time and help.

Always remember to work in a well-ventilated room, assess your young crafter's propensity to put small objects into his or her mouth (choose materials accordingly), and work with nontoxic materials. Remember that younger siblings may pick up odds and ends from the floor or pull items off the table's edge. When scissors are used, please use child safety scissors, never sharp adult scissors.

When you "reach your destination," send lots of postcards back home. Also pay a visit to your local library and log on to the World Wide Web to learn more about the places you visited. Kids are experts at flights of imagination, which makes them wonderful travelers — real or pretend!

Your Friend

Away We Go!

Hooray! We're off on a journey around the world! Together we'll visit all **seven continents** and cross **four oceans**. We'll travel to different countries to meet a lot of children, share their customs, and learn about their parts of the world.

Kids around the world have different skin colors, different religions, and different interests, and they enjoy different foods. But just like you, they like to play, they like to have pets, and they like to have parties and celebrate holidays. And every one of them is important, just like you!

So let's get ready to travel around the globe to learn about other people and places. We'll learn about some of the areas in which they live, some of the musical instruments they play, and some of the animals that live near them. We'll also explore ancient wonders (like the mysterious statues on Easter Island) and visit modern marvels (like the Eiffel Tower in Paris). We'll see sand dunes in the desert and penguins in the snow. We'll go to museums and monuments, castles and islands. What an adventure!

The route we travel will take us around the globe. You can follow this route, or you can turn to any place or activity that interests you. Use your passport (see page 7) to keep track of the places you visit and your suitcase (see page 8) to hold some of the crafts you make. Remember, our world is not so large. The more we learn about it, the more exciting it is.

Bon voyage! (Have a great trip!)

Miss Judy

Prepare Your Passport

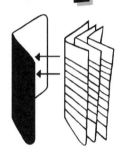

Hi!
I received my passport today!
It is like a book with my picture
in it. I have to show my passport
whenever I enter a new country. When
I arrive, someone will stamp it with an
official seal and the date. I'll have lots of
stamps in my passport when I get home!

Your Friend

What you need:

- Cereal-box cardboard
- Child safety scissors
- Pencil
- Blue construction paper
- Glue stick
- White paper
- Stapler (for grown-up use only)
- Your photo (ask to use)
- Black marker
- Stars (optional)

What you do:

1. Cut out a 5" x 7" (13 x 18 cm) rectangle from the cardboard. Ask a grown-up to help you trace the cardboard onto blue paper and cut around the traced line.

2. Glue the blue paper onto the cardboard. Fold the cardboard in half as shown.

3. Cut out a 4.5" x 6.5" (11 x 16 cm) rectangle from the cardboard. Trace the cardboard onto white paper three times. Cut out all three pieces and fold them in half the short way.

4. Have a grown-up help you staple the white paper inside the blue cardboard cover. Glue your photo inside the passport. Use the marker to write "Passport" on the front cover. Glue on stars.

Pack a Suitcase

What you need:

- Empty cardboard cereal box
- Child safety scissors
- Scrap of cereal-box cardboard
- Brown paper grocery bag
- Transparent tape
- Masking tape
- 2 paper fasteners*
- Rubber band
- Brown tempera paint, in dish or lid
- Paintbrush
- Decorations (optional)

*Paper fasteners pose a choking and poking danger to young children. Adults should control the supply and insert them into the project.

What you do:

1. Cut around three sides of the cereal box's front panel as shown. Cut out a handle from the scrap cardboard.

2. Wrap the box and the handle in the brown paper. Tape to hold.

3. Use masking tape to attach the handle to the side panel of the box. Loosely attach paper fasteners to the top and front panels of the suitcase.

4. Wrap a rubber band around the paper fasteners to close the suitcase.

5. Decorate your suitcase by painting on brown straps, or adding stickers or pictures of the things you meet in your travels.

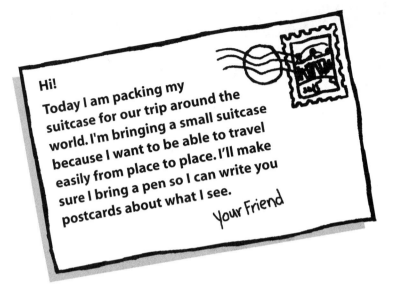

Hi!

Today I am packing my suitcase for our trip around the world. I'm bringing a small suitcase because I want to be able to travel easily from place to place. I'll make sure I bring a pen so I can write you postcards about what I see.

Your Friend

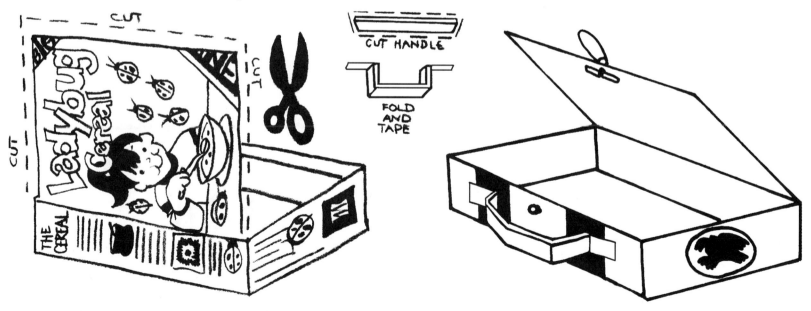

Map of the World

All packed and passport ready? Let's get started on our journey! Throughout the trip, we can use this map to tell us where in the world we are. A map is a picture showing the shape and location of a place as if you were looking down from high in the sky. A map shows you where you are now and where you're going next. A map is a wonderful tool!

Our map will help us find all of the continents we're going to visit, along with the oceans we'll cross to visit them. A *continent* is a huge area of land. Nearby islands are often considered part of a continent. The seven continents on earth are *North America*, *Australia* and many nearby islands, *Asia, Africa, Europe, South* and *Central America,* and *Antarctica.* Some continents are connected to other continents (for example, Asia and Europe), while others are completely surrounded by oceans (Australia, for instance). Isn't it amazing what you can learn from a map?

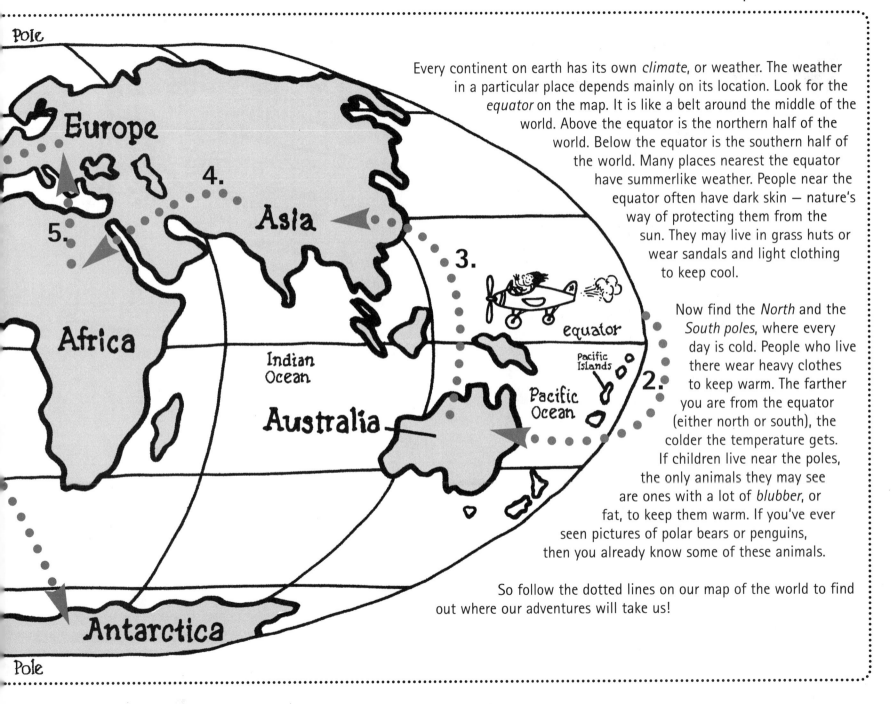

Pole

Europe

5.

4.

Asia

Africa

Indian
Ocean

Australia

Pacific
Islands

Pacific
Ocean

equator

3.

2.

Antarctica

Pole

Every continent on earth has its own *climate*, or weather. The weather in a particular place depends mainly on its location. Look for the *equator* on the map. It is like a belt around the middle of the world. Above the equator is the northern half of the world. Below the equator is the southern half of the world. Many places nearest the equator have summerlike weather. People near the equator often have dark skin — nature's way of protecting them from the sun. They may live in grass huts or wear sandals and light clothing to keep cool.

Now find the *North* and the *South poles*, where every day is cold. People who live there wear heavy clothes to keep warm. The farther you are from the equator (either north or south), the colder the temperature gets. If children live near the poles, the only animals they may see are ones with a lot of *blubber*, or fat, to keep them warm. If you've ever seen pictures of polar bears or penguins, then you already know some of these animals.

So follow the dotted lines on our map of the world to find out where our adventures will take us!

Save Your Postage Stamps

Hello!

Did you know that every country has its own postage stamps with different designs, colors, and shapes? You can keep the stamps that are sent to you to start a stamp collection!

Your Friend

What you need:

- Cereal-box cardboard
- Child safety scissors
- Pencil
- Assorted construction paper (including white)
- Wavy-edged child safety scissors
- Glue stick
- Markers

What you do:

1. Cut out a 3" x 3 1/2" (7.5 x 8.5 cm) shape from the cardboard. Ask a grown-up to help you trace the cardboard shape onto the white construction paper. Using the wavy-edged scissors, cut out the shapes to make stamps.

2. Cut out a 2" x 2 1/2" (5 x 6 cm) shape from the cardboard. Ask a grown-up to help you trace this cardboard shape onto assorted light-colored paper. Cut them out.

3. Glue a colored piece onto each white, wavy-edged stamp. Use markers to decorate the stamps with boats, flowers, or anything you want.

North America

Welcome to North America! This big continent is named after *Amerigo Vespucci*, an early explorer of the continent. There are three countries on this continent: *Canada* is at the top, *Mexico* is at the bottom, and the *United States* is in the middle. People at the top of North America live near the North Pole, so their weather is often very cold with very long winters. People in southern Canada and the United States live in all sorts of climates. There are cold, snowy mountains and beautiful seashores, and in the U.S., hot, sandy deserts. People in Mexico live near the equator. They have very warm weather, beautiful beaches, and deserts, but high, cool mountains, too.

North America

Statue of Liberty Torch

Hi!
Today I visited this famous statue that welcomes people from across the Atlantic Ocean to the United States in North America! There are steps *inside* her so you can climb to the top — up to the gigantic crown on her forehead. I climbed 354 steps (whew)! I was *tired!*

Your Friend

What you need:

- Child safety scissors
- Paper cup
- Aluminum foil
- Cardboard paper-towel tube
- Green, red, and yellow construction paper
- Transparent tape

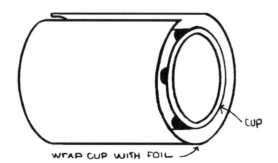

CUT BOTTOM FROM CUP

CUP

WRAP CUP WITH FOIL

What you do:

1. Cut away a large circle from the bottom of the paper cup. Wrap the cup in aluminum foil.

2. Wrap the tube in green construction paper. Tape to hold. Slide the tube through the hole in the cup. Tape to hold.

3. Tear strips of yellow and red paper. Tape them around the top of the tube for flames.

Site:
**Ellis Island,
New York City, New York,
United States**

⚙ **Make a Statue of Liberty Crown.** Cut out the center of a large paper plate. Glue eight green construction paper triangles around the rim. Now, pose like the real Statue of Liberty!

⚙ **Learn More!** Visit this website to learn more about the Statue of Liberty: **www.endex.com/gf/ buildings/liberty/ liberty.html**

Spirit of St. Louis

Hello!

Charles Lindbergh was the first person to fly a plane from one continent across an ocean to another continent. His plane was called the *Spirit of St. Louis.* He flew it from North America to Europe. His plane is in a museum now, where I saw it hanging from the ceiling. It looked small for such a long trip!   Your Friend

REAR PROPELLER

SPIRIT of ST. LOUIS

What you need:

- Transparent tape
- Pint (500 ml) milk carton
- Construction paper
- Cereal-box cardboard
- Child safety scissors
- 4 Popsicle sticks
- Marker

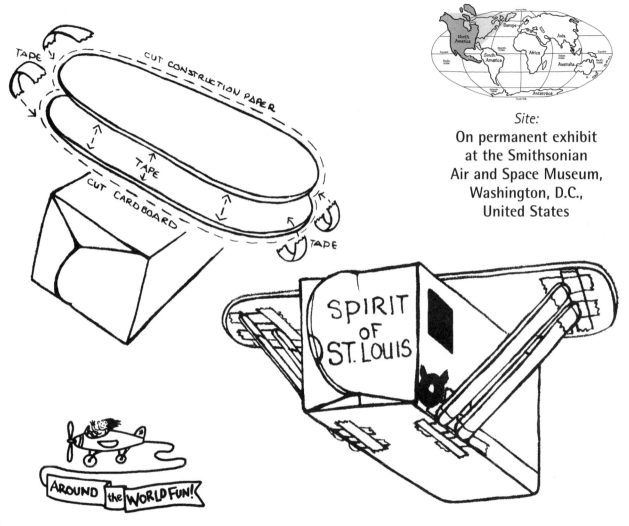

Site:
**On permanent exhibit
at the Smithsonian
Air and Space Museum,
Washington, D.C.,
United States**

What you do:

1. Tape closed the lid of the milk carton. Wrap the carton in construction paper. Tape to hold.

2. Cut out a piece for the plane's wings from the cardboard. Cover the top of the piece with construction paper. Tape the wings to the top of the carton.

3. Tape the ends of two Popsicle sticks to the underside of one wing and to the carton as shown. Repeat for second wing.

4. Cut out the rear propeller from the cardboard and tape it to the plane. Use the marker to draw the plane's windows, wheels, and front propeller.

⚙ **Map Talk.** Look at the map on pages 10-11. If Charles Lindbergh flew from North America to Europe, what ocean did he cross? Where in the world would *you* like to fly?

⚙ **Talk About It.** Do you have a dream about what you'd like to do when you grow up, like fly an airplane? Tell a story about your dream to a grown-up, who can write it down for you. Then, draw a picture of your dream!

Hatching Alligator

Howdy!

This morning we hiked along a trail in the Everglades. We had to hike in the morning because it is so hot here. I saw a big mound of dirt that turned out to be an alligator's nest. I didn't get too close!

Your Friend

What you need:

- Black construction paper
- Child safety scissors
- Sponge (small piece)
- Yellow tempera paint, in a dish or lid
- Small white paper plate
- Glue stick
- Paper fastener*

Paper fasteners pose a choking and poking danger to young children. Adults should control the supply and insert them into the project.

What you do:

1. Cut out a baby alligator from the black paper. Dab the sponge into the paint. Press it onto the alligator to make a skin design. Let dry.

2. Holding the paper plate upside down, cut a zigzag line across the center. Separate the two halves.

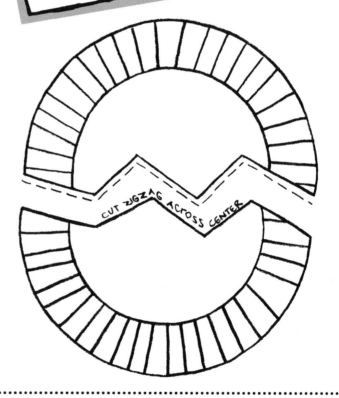

CUT ZIGZAG ACROSS CENTER

3. Glue the alligator inside the lower half of the plate as shown. Use the paper fastener to attach the plate halves together so the halves can be raised and lowered.

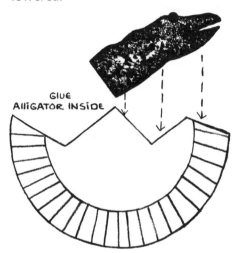

GLUE
ALLIGATOR INSIDE

PAPER FASTENER

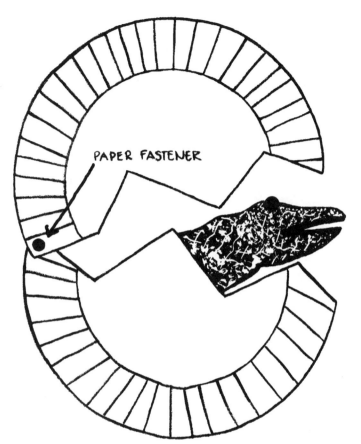

Site:
Found in the Everglades National Park in southwestern Florida. The Mississippi, or American, alligator is found in the southeastern United States. The Chinese alligator is found in the Yangtze River region of China.

AROUND the WORLD FUN!

⚙ **Camouflage Game.** It's hard to see alligators because their skin is the color of mud and water. That's called *camouflage* — when your color blends into your surroundings. Take a walk with a grown-up and look very carefully at what you see. Do you see anything almost hidden because of its camouflage colors? How about a green bug on a green leaf or a gray squirrel on a gray branch?

⚙ **How Do They Do It?** Do you know how an alligator can see above the water when its body is below the water? Its eyes stick up above its skull! Can you think of other animals that have odd traits that enable them to see, hear, or eat? How about a giraffe that has a long neck to eat leaves in the trees?

The Dinosaur "Sue"

What you do:

1. Cut away the rim of the plate. Cut around the plate in a continuous spiral for a thin strip as shown.

2. Cut out dino bones from the spiral strip. Cut out a dino skull from the center of the plate.

3. Glue the bones and skull onto the black paper.

What you need:

- Child safety scissors
- Styrofoam paper plate
- Black construction paper
- White craft glue

Wow!

Today I saw the dinosaur named "Sue," a Tyrannosaurus rex whose bones were found in the middle of North America. It lived there more than 60 million years ago. "Sue" is so huge that I felt like a tiny ant next to her!

Your Friend

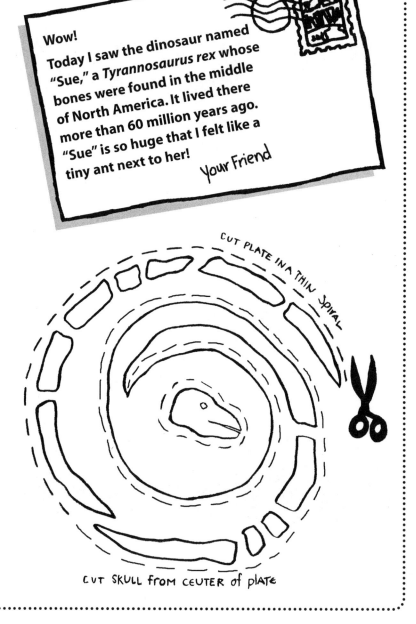

CUT PLATE IN A THIN SPIRAL

CUT SKULL FROM CENTER OF PLATE

Site:
**On permanent
exhibit at the
Field Museum in
Chicago, Illinois,
United States**

⚙ **Learn More!** Check out
this website about Sue:
www.fmnh.org/sue/

⚙ **Story Corner.** Read
*The Field Mouse and the
Dinosaur Named Sue*
by Jan Wahl.

Papel Picado

What you need:

- Sheet of tissue paper
- Child safety scissors
- String or yarn
- White craft glue

¡Hola!

A *papel picado* is a colorful paper decoration that hangs like a banner in Mexican marketplaces. Sometimes, many layers of paper are stacked together. Then, many *papel picados* can be cut at one time. They sure are fun to see and fun to make!

Your Friend

ACCORDION-FOLD PAPER

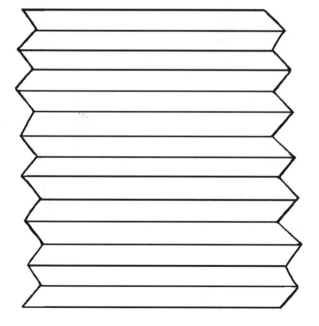

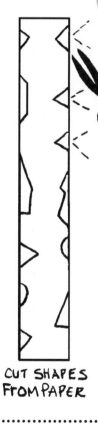

CUT SHAPES FROM PAPER

What you do:

1. Lay the tissue paper flat. Accordion-fold the paper in 1" (2.5 cm) folds.

2. Cut shapes and designs along the folds 1" (2.5 cm) from the top as shown. Open the paper to see the design.

3. Fold the top edge of the tissue paper over the string and glue to hold. When dry, hang the papel picado from the string.

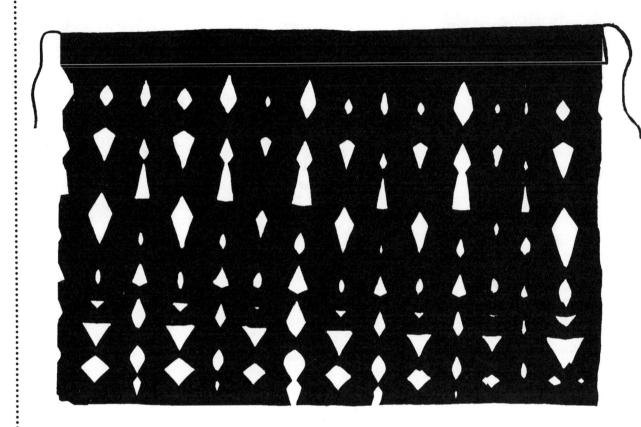

Site:
Popular throughout Mexico and wherever Mexican people live, such as in the southwestern United States

⚙ **Fiesta Time!** A *fiesta* (a festival) is a time to celebrate with family and friends. Here's an easy recipe for *tacos* (which make a light meal or a snack): Ask a grown-up to brown in a large skillet 1 lb (500 g) of ground beef and a small onion, chopped. Stir in $1/4$ teaspoon (1 ml) cumin, $1/2$ teaspoon (2 ml) oregano, and $1/2$ teaspoon (2 ml) garlic powder. Heat taco shells according to the directions on the package. Spoon about $1/4$ cup (50 ml) of the taco filling into each shell. Top with shredded cheese and lettuce. *Delicioso!*

⚙ **Learn More!** Read the book *Fiesta!* by Ginger Foglesong Guy to learn to count in Spanish.

Giant Sequoia

Hello!

Can you imagine this? I saw a tree so tall that you can't even see the top of it! And its trunk is so wide that you can't reach all the way around it! These trees are called *giant sequoias*. I won't try climbing one of these!

Your Friend

What you need:

- Paper cup
- Child safety scissors
- Brown and green construction paper
- Transparent tape
- Cardboard paper-towel tube
- Brown or black marker

What you do:

1. Cut away a large circle from the bottom of the paper cup. Wrap the cup in brown construction paper and tape to hold.

2. Roll the tube in brown construction paper, leaving 4" (10 cm) hanging over one end. Tape to hold. Cut the paper end into strips as shown and bend them back for the tree's branches.

3. Hold the cup upside down and insert the tube into the hole cut out from the bottom. Use a marker to draw the tree's bark.

4. Cut out leaves from the green construction paper. Tape them onto the branches on top.

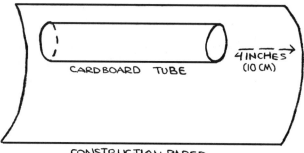

CARDBOARD TUBE   4 INCHES (10 CM)

CONSTRUCTION PAPER

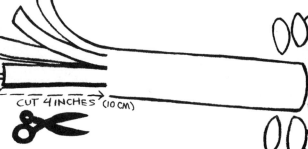

CUT 4 INCHES (10 CM)

Site:
Found in a narrow band along the west coast of North America, from southwestern Oregon to Monterey, California, United States

❋ **Beautiful Leaves!** Take a walk with a grown-up and point out the different kinds of trees in your neighborhood. Pick up leaves along the way. How many different shapes do you see?

Totem Pole

What you need:

- Cardboard paper-towel tube
- Brown construction paper
- Transparent tape
- Assorted markers
- Child safety scissors
- Cereal-box cardboard

Greetings!

Today I saw real totem poles that the native people carved from trees. Faces and figures are carved on top of one another. Totem poles tell stories about a family. I wish we had a family totem pole. We could tell lots of funny stories!

Your Friend

What you do:

1. Wrap the tube in the brown paper. Tape to hold.

2. Use markers to draw faces and geometric designs on the totem pole.

3. Cut four slits in the bottom of the tube. Cut out four "feet" from the cereal-box cardboard. Slide the "feet" into the slits as shown. Tape to hold.

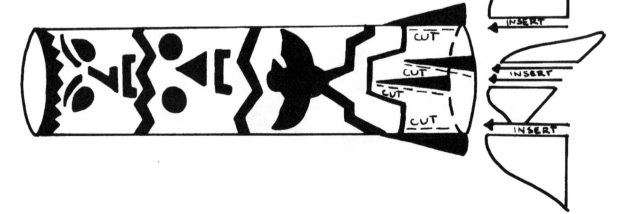

Site:
**Located in
Thunderbird Park,
Victoria,
British Columbia,
Canada. Totem poles
can also be seen
up and down the
northwest coast
of the United States
and Canada.**

⚙ **Tell a Family Story.** Make a family totem pole. Draw the people and the places important to you. (If you need more room, use two tubes). When you are done, ask your family and friends if they recognize the story.

⚙ **Tell a Story in Three Ways.** *Draw* a picture, *act* it out (can anyone guess what the story is about?), and then *use words* to tell the story to your family and friends. Is it a happy story or a sad one?

Bald Eagle

What you need:

- White construction paper
- Child safety scissors
- Yellow and brown markers
- 2 brown paper lunch bags
- Transparent tape

Hi!
Today I watched a bald eagle swoop across a river and catch a fish in its *talons* (claws). The bald eagle's bill is bright yellow. It has a white head. That's what makes it look bald! Its tail feathers are white, too.

Your Friend

YELLOW

FRINGE

TAPE WINGS UNDERNEATH FLAP

What you do:

1. Cut out the eagle's head and tail feathers from the white paper. Cut fringe around the head for feathers. Color the eagle's beak yellow.

2. Tape the eagle's head onto the flap of the first bag. Cut out the eagle's wings from the second bag and tape them underneath the flap as shown.

3. Tape the eagle's tail feathers to the back of the bag. Use the brown marker to draw on feathers and an eye.

TAPE FEATHERS TO BAG

TAIL FEATHERS

Site:
Found only in North America near coastlines, rivers, lakes, and coastal pinelands from Alaska and Canada south into Florida and Baja California

AROUND the WORLD FUN!

✪ **Pretend Play.** The bald eagle's wingspan is 7' (2 m). Wow! With wings that big, the eagle can fly gracefully for long periods of time. Your eagle can fly, too! Put your hand inside the bag to make a puppet. Glide gracefully around the room as your eagle floats on air.

✪ **Learn More!** To learn more about this majestic American bird, check out this website: **www.eagles.org**

The Pacific Islands and Australia

The Pacific Ocean is the largest ocean on the earth, and it is so full of small islands that it's almost impossible to count them all! It's easy to find Australia, though; it is the smallest continent but one of the largest countries on earth! It is between the Pacific and Indian oceans, along with many other island countries. There are lots of strange and funny animals in Australia and the Pacific Islands! Can you think of any that you know about already? If you don't, you're sure to meet some on this trip!

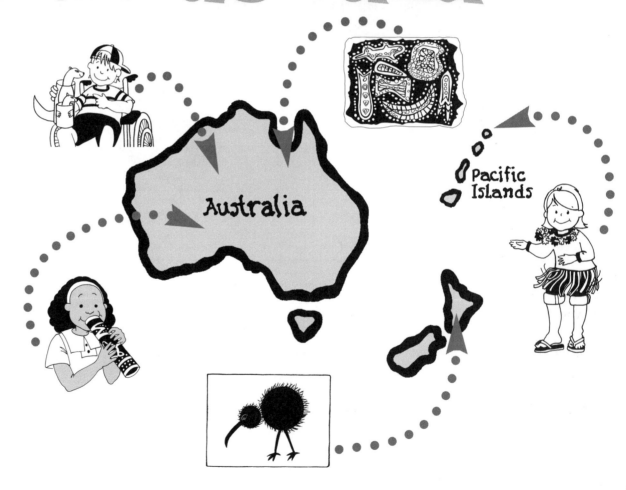

Australia

Pacific Islands

Beautiful Lei

Aloha!

To welcome me to Hawaii, friends put a necklace of flowers, called a lei, around my neck. That's how Hawaiians greet people. They make the necklaces from the beautiful flowers that grow on the islands. I liked the necklace because it was pretty and smelled beautiful. *Your Friend*

What you need:

- Assorted construction paper
- Child safety scissors
- Hole punch
- Yarn (enough to make a long necklace)
- Tape
- Tube pasta

What you do:

1. Cut out shapes of flowers from construction paper. Punch a hole in the center of each flower.

2. Put a piece of tape on the yarn end. Thread the flowers onto the yarn, alternating each flower with a piece of pasta. Remove the tape. Tie the ends of the yarn together for a long necklace.

CONTINUED...

Site:
**Hawaiian Islands
in
Pacific Ocean**

⚙ **Play Meet and Greet.** Around the world there are many different ways to greet people.

- In **North America**, people mostly shake hands.
- In **Europe**, French people often kiss one another on each cheek.
- In **Africa**, Bedouin men stroke their beards.
- In **Africa**, Egyptian people often kiss three times: first on one cheek, then the other, then back to the first cheek.
- In **Asia**, Japanese people often bow to one another.
- In **South America**, Aymara women in Bolivia tip their bowler hats.

Now play Meet and Greet. Greet your family members and friends in some of the ways above. Which way do you like best?

Kiwi Bird

What you need:

- Styrofoam tray (from fruits or vegetables only)
- Child safety scissors
- Cereal-box cardboard
- Tacky glue
- Brown poster paint, in a dish or lid
- Paintbrush
- Light-colored paper
- Brown marker

What you do:

1. From the tray, cut out a small circle for the head and a medium-sized circle for the body. Cut out a long piece for the beak and two straight pieces for the legs.

2. Glue the pieces onto the cardboard to make a kiwi as shown. Allow to dry.

Greetings,

Wow! Today I saw kiwi birds, and they're awesome! And guess what? Kiwi birds of New Zealand have no tails. They have hairlike feathers, but cannot fly. They sleep all day, never drink a drop of water, are nearly blind, and use their nostrils to smell worms buried under the dirt.

Your Friend

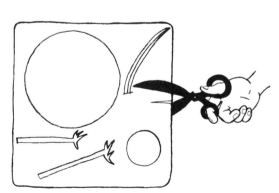

CONTINUED...

3. Brush a thin layer of paint over the Styrofoam bird. Press the paper on top of the painted bird and gently rub. Lift the paper and let the print dry.

4. Use the marker to draw on the kiwi's eyes and feathers.

Lift

After rubbing PAPER ON PAINTED Bird Lift AND LET DRY

Site:
**The forests of
New Zealand**

⚙ **Symbols.** The kiwi bird is the national symbol of New Zealand. Can you name the bird that is the national symbol of the United States? If you said the bald eagle (see page 28), you're right!

⚙ **Kiwis!** Sometimes when we hear the word "kiwi," we think of the *kiwifruit*, which is grown in New Zealand. Eat a kiwifruit. Is it sweet or tart?

Aboriginal Bark Painting

What you need:

- Brown paper grocery bag
- Assorted construction paper (including black)
- Glue stick
- Child safety scissors
- Pencil with eraser
- White tempera paint, in a dish or lid
- Black marker

What you do:

1. Cut open the paper bag and lay it flat. Tear a large piece of brown paper from the bag.

2. Tear the black paper in the same shape, slightly smaller than the brown paper. Glue the black paper onto the brown paper.

3. Cut out shapes from the other colors of construction paper. Glue them onto the black paper.

4. Dip the eraser into the paint. Then, press dots on and around the shapes. Use the marker to decorate the shapes.

G'day!

These paintings are made on eucalyptus tree bark. *Aboriginal* (native) paintings are often of animals, plants, and humans. My favorite part of the painting is the dots!

Your Friend

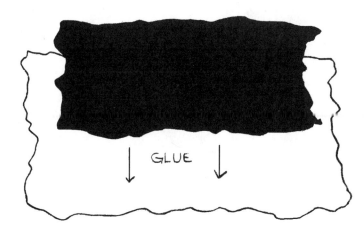

GLUE

 CONTINUED...

Site:
**Australia,
home of the
Aborigines,
the native peoples**

✪ **Dream Time.** Use your
bark painting to tell a
story. Your story could be
about a dream you had.
Or tell a story about your
favorite pet, a visit to the
zoo, or fun with your
friends.

Didgeridoo

What you need:

- Cardboard paper-towel tube (for a longer instrument, use a gift-wrap tube)
- White tempera paint, in a dish or lid
- Thin paintbrush

G'day!

We enjoyed a concert of Aboriginal dance and music. We listened to the sound of the *didgeridoo*. Some people believe it is the world's oldest wind instrument (that's any instrument that you blow into, like a flute)! It's made from parts of the eucalyptus tree. I clapped my hands along with the music. It was so much fun!

Your Friend

What you do:

1. Use white paint to create Aboriginal-like designs on your tube. Allow to dry.

SAMPLE ABORIGINAL DESIGN

SAMPLE ABORIGINAL DESIGN

CONTINUED...

Site:
Australia

⚙ **Play the Didgeridoo.**
Puff out your cheeks and push out your lips. Next, press your lips up against the cardboard-tube didgeridoo and blow air through your lips so they vibrate. You should be making a low-pitched, buzzing sound.

⚙ **Make Music!** Ask a friend to clap two sticks of wood together to accompany your didgeridoo. Now, dance or move to the music!

Kangaroo

G'day!

Hop, hop, hop. That's how the kangaroo I saw today got around. (And I hopped up and down, too!). A baby kangaroo is called a "joey." Every mother kangaroo carries her baby in her pouch. That's how the joey stays warm and dry. What a way to travel!

Your Friend

What you do:

1. Cut open the paper bag. Wrap the cardboard tubes in the brown paper. Tape to hold.

2. Ask a grown-up to staple the tubes together as shown.

3. Cut out kangaroo heads (one large, one small) and a tail from construction paper. Use the marker to draw on the eyes, nose, and mouth of the mother kangaroo and the joey.

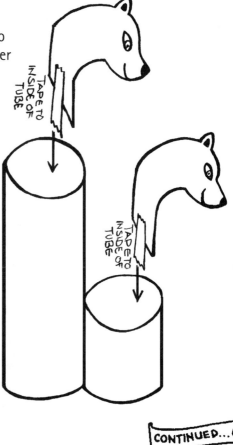

TAPE TO INSIDE OF TUBE

TAPE TO INSIDE OF TUBE

What you need:

- Brown paper lunch bag
- Child safety scissors
- 1 $\frac{1}{2}$ cardboard toilet-paper tubes
- Transparent tape
- Stapler (for grown-up use only)
- Brown construction paper
- Black marker

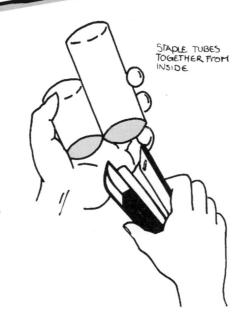

STAPLE TUBES TOGETHER FROM INSIDE

CONTINUED...

4. Tape the large head to the long tube; tape the small head to the short tube. Tape the tail onto the side of the tube. Draw the mother kangaroo's arms around the joey.

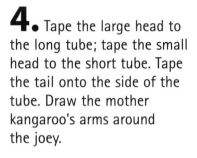

Site:
Australia, Tasmania, and New Guinea

⚙ **"Kangaroo Crossing."** Yes, these signs actually are found on roads in the Australian bush! Make crossing signs by cutting out a triangle from cereal-box cardboard. Use markers to draw a kangaroo on each sign. Put them up around your house and hop by the signs!

⚙ **Story Corner.** Read the book *Katy No Pocket* by Emmy Payne.

Asia

Have you ever heard of *Japan*, *China*, or *India?* They are countries in Asia. People who live in Asia are called Asians. Asia is the world's largest continent on earth! It's also the youngest continent. That means it was the last one to be formed.

And guess what? The highest place on earth and the lowest place on earth are both in Asia! Mount Everest is the highest mountain in the world, and the Dead Sea is the lowest point in the world.

Asia has many islands, which is why it has more coastline than any other continent. Just think of all the beaches you could visit and all the fish you could eat!

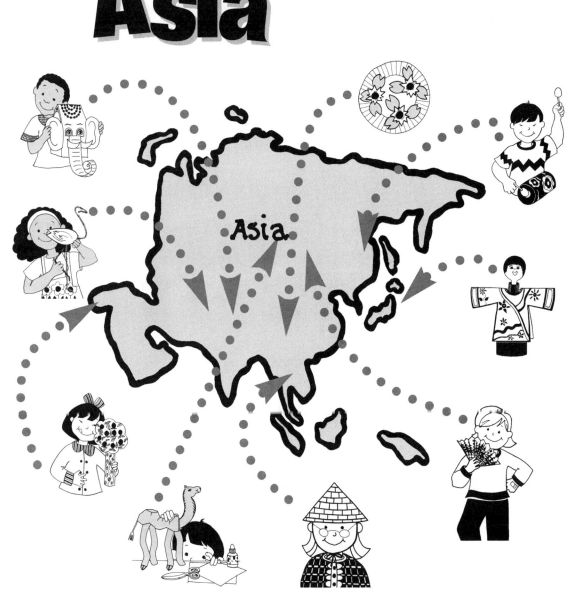

Japanese Doll

What you need:

- Cereal-box cardboard
- Child safety scissors
- Pencil
- Assorted construction paper
- Glue stick
- Assorted markers
- Plastic bottle, about 16-oz. (500 ml) size
- Transparent tape

Konichiwa!

I saw so many beautiful dolls today! Parents and daughters celebrate the Doll Festival in Japan. Dolls are displayed on a platform covered with red felt. Many of the dolls are dressed in lovely silk *kimonos* (traditional Japanese clothes) that are made in Asia.

Your Friend

What you do:

1. Cut out the doll's head and long neck from the cardboard. Ask a grown-up to help you trace it onto construction paper two times. Glue the pieces to both sides of the cardboard head. Use markers to draw the doll's face on one side; draw hair on the other side.

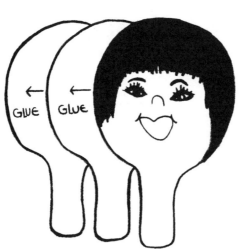

2. Wrap the bottle in construction paper and tape to hold. Pinch the paper together at the neck of the bottle.

3. Fold a piece of construction paper in half and cut out a T shape for the doll's kimono. Use the markers to decorate it. Cut a small slit in the top of the fold, and place the kimono over the neck of the bottle.

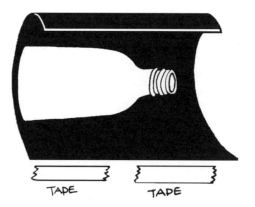

4. Glue the kimono to the front and back of the bottle and glue the sleeves together. Insert the doll's head into the bottle.

FOLD

SMALL SLIT FOR bottle NECK

GLUE BOTTOM OF THE SLEEVES TOGETHER

GLUE THE KIMONO TO THE FRONT AND BACK OF THE BOTTLE

Site:
Made and displayed in Japan, though other kinds of dolls are found all over the world

AROUND the WORLD FUN!

⚙ **Gather Flowers.** Japan's Doll Festival is held when the peach blossoms are in bloom. Branches of the blossoms are placed on the display. Gather a bunch of flowers and place them alongside your dolls, Japanese-style.

⚙ **Smooth as Silk!** The making and weaving of silk material began in Asia about 5,000 years ago! Ask a grown-up to show you anything made of silk, like a necktie or a scarf. What does it feel like — smooth, soft, or rough?

⚙ **Special Days.** Japanese children also display their dolls on *Children's Day*. Are there any special days in your country that are planned for children, parents, or grandparents?

Korean Drum

What you need:

What you do:

- Round cardboard carton with lid (oatmeal, cornmeal, or bread-crumb container)
- Assorted construction paper
- Transparent tape
- Pencil
- Child safety scissors
- Glue stick
- Decorations

1. Wrap the carton in construction paper. Tape to hold. Cut off the excess on both ends.

2. Ask a grown-up to help you trace the end of the carton onto the paper two times. Cut out each circle and glue one to each end of the carton.

3. Cut out paper decorations and glue them onto the carton.

Annyong ha shimnikka!

Korean drums lie on their sides so the drummer can hit both ends. The sound of the drum goes *boom, boom, boom*. The one I heard sounded very loud. Sometimes when the drum was too loud I covered my ears with my hands.

Your Friend

GLUE TOGETHER

GLUE TOGETHER

Around the World Fun!

⚙ **Make Different Sounds**. Korean drummers sometimes use their hands to play their drums, and they also use drumsticks. Play your drum with your fingertips. Then, make a ball out of clay and stick an unsharpened pencil into it. Lay your drum on its side and tap the ends with your clay-and-pencil drumstick. For a tasty drumstick, poke a thin pretzel stick into a marshmallow! Listen to the sound it makes and then eat it up!

Site:
Specific to Korea and Japan, though many kinds of drums are found on every continent around the world

Bactrian Camel

Ni hao?

I rode a camel today! It was a very bumpy ride. I don't think I'd like to ride all the way across the desert on one! Camels can travel across the desert in Asia because they can survive without water for many days. That's not the life for me — I need food and water many times a day!

Your Friend

What you do:

1. Cut out a two-cup section from the egg carton for the body. Cut out two 1" x 11" (2.5 x 28 cm) strips from the cardboard as shown for the legs.

2. Turn the egg cups upside down and paint them brown. Paint one side of both of the cardboard strips brown. Allow to dry.

What you need:

- Cardboard egg carton
- Child safety scissors
- Cereal-box cardboard
- Brown tempera paint, in a dish or lid
- Paintbrush
- Brown construction paper
- Brown marker
- Tacky glue

CUT OUT TWO CUPS FROM EGG CARTON

CUT STRIPS OF CARDBOARD FOR LEGS →

3. Cut out the camel's head, neck, and tail from the brown paper. Use the marker to draw on the eyes, nose, and mouth.

4. Cut a slit in the end of the egg carton and insert the camel's neck. Glue to hold. Glue on the tail. Bend the legs and glue them into the egg cups. Use the marker to draw on the feet.

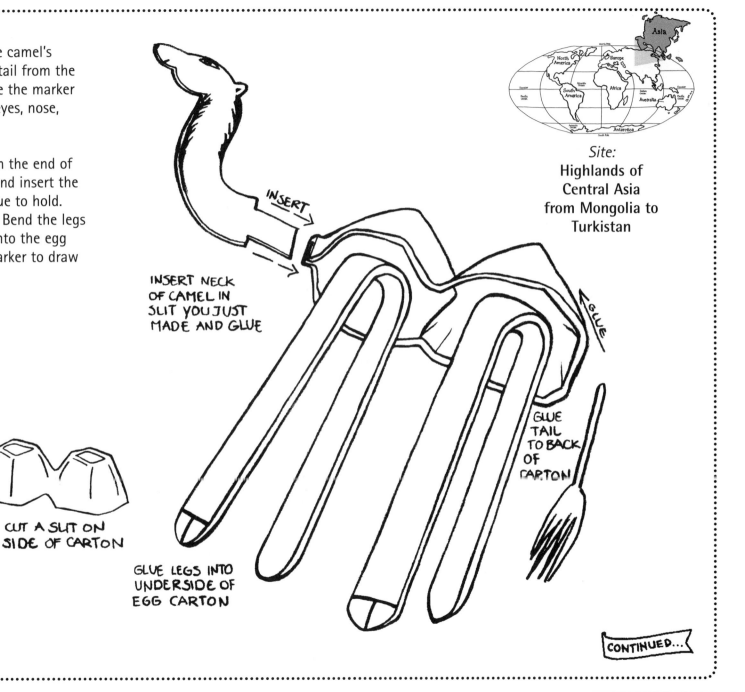

Site:
Highlands of Central Asia from Mongolia to Turkistan

INSERT

INSERT NECK OF CAMEL IN SLIT YOU JUST MADE AND GLUE

GLUE

GLUE TAIL TO BACK OF CARTON

CUT

CUT A SLIT ON SIDE OF CARTON

GLUE LEGS INTO UNDERSIDE OF EGG CARTON

CONTINUED...

AROUND the WORLD FUN!

✺ **The Better to See You.**
Camels' eyes have double rows of eyelashes. How do you think this helps them when the desert sand blows? What do you do to protect your eyes from the sun?

✺ **Meet a New Creature.**
Yaks (large, shaggy-haired oxen) are another kind of animal found in Asia. They are very strong and can pull heavy loads. Yaks carry their heads so low that their noses almost touch the ground. How low do you have to bend to touch your nose to the ground? Take a yak-walk around the room.

Chinese Paper Fan

Ni hao?

Today I went to the zoo to see giant pandas. It sure was hot outside! My friend let me use her Chinese fan to cool off. She had a beautiful paper fan with a lovely painting on it. Her brother had a bamboo fan with a design carved in it.

Your Friend

What you need:

- Large piece of white paper
- Assorted markers
- Transparent tape

What you do:

1. Hold the paper so the long side is on the bottom. Use colorful markers to draw a picture on the top half.

2. Turn the paper around and draw a picture on the other half.

CONTINUED...

3. Accordion-fold the paper. Pinch the pleated paper in the center. Bring up the two sides and tape together for a fan.

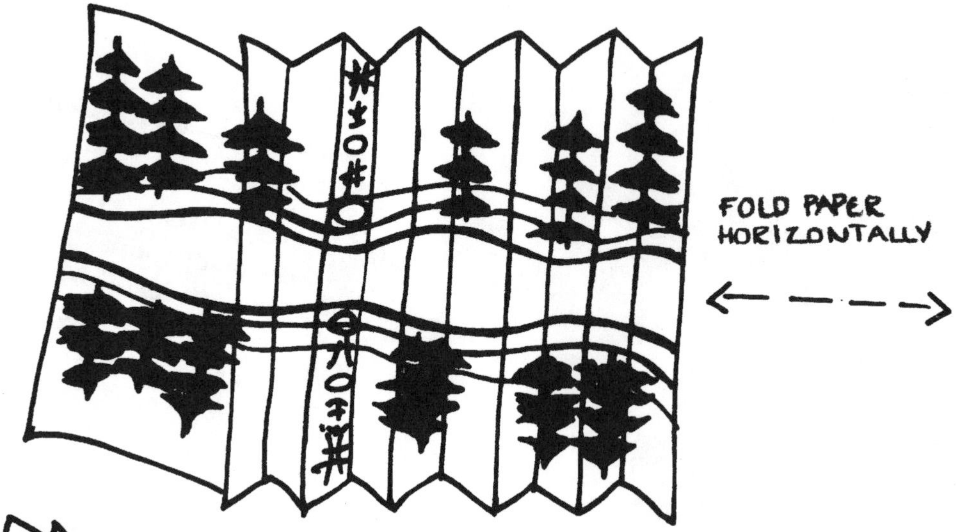

FOLD PAPER HORIZONTALLY

←– – –→

TAPE

CONTINUED...

HOLD FAN FOR EVERYONE TO SEE

AROUND the WORLD FUN!

Site:
Used in China, though all kinds of fans are used all over the world in hot weather

⚙ **Keeping Cool.** On hot days in China, both men and women use a paper fan, or *shan*, to cool off. How do you cool off on a hot day? Do you go for a swim? Sit under a leafy tree? Drink glasses of ice-cold lemonade?

⚙ **Eating with Sticks.** In many parts of Asia, people eat with chopsticks. Try eating some of your favorite foods with chopsticks. If you don't have chopsticks, use two Popsicle sticks. See how the fingers hold the sticks in the picture? Can you pick up raisins? Strawberries? Spaghetti?

Conical Hat

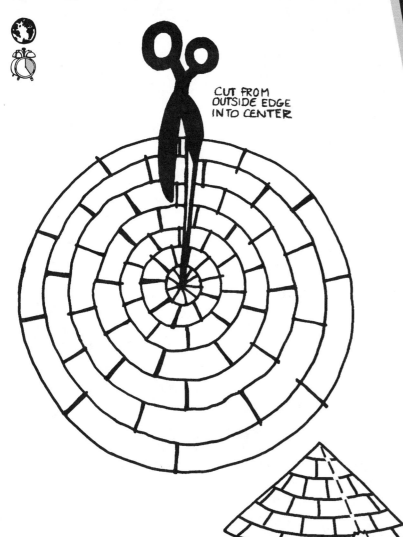

CUT FROM OUTSIDE EDGE INTO CENTER

Danh to!

The sun can get very strong and hot here in Asia. I'm wearing a *non la*, a Vietnamese hat that has a point at the top. It ties under my chin and keeps the hot sun off my face.

Your Friend

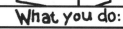

What you do:

1. Cut open the bag and lay it flat. Cut out a 13" (33 cm) wide circle from the bag.

2. Use the marker to draw a woven pattern on the hat.

3. Make a cut from the outside edge of the circle into the center. Overlap the edges to form a peak. Tape the slit ends together.

4. Tape one piece of yarn to each side of the hat to make two ties.

What you need:

- Brown paper grocery bag
- Child safety scissors
- Brown marker
- Transparent tape
- Yarn

Site:
**Vietnam,
Southeast Asia,
and parts of
southern China**

✿ **Hats for Today!** How many different kinds of hats do you have? Count them up and sort them into winter and summer hats. For fun, take a piece of newspaper and some tape to make yourself a special, one-of-a-kind hat. Then, gather your friends or family, put on hats, and have a parade playing your Korean drum (see page 44).

Lotus Flower

What you need:

- Large white paper plate
- Blue tempera paint, in a dish or lid
- Paintbrush
- Styrofoam egg carton
- Child safety scissors
- Orange and green construction paper
- Tacky glue

Sawasdee!

It's so beautiful here in Asia! I saw yellow, purple, white, pink, and red lotus flowers growing in ponds today. It is a favorite flower in Thailand. In fact, some girls in Asia are named after the lotus blossom.

Your Friend

What you do:

1. Paint the plate blue. Allow to dry.

2. Cut out cups from the egg carton. Cut around the edges to make petals. Glue a dot of orange paper in the center of each flower. Glue the flowers onto the plate.

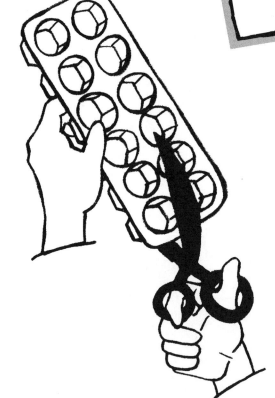

CUT AROUND EGG CUPS TO FORM PETALS

3. Cut out lotus leaves (see the shape in the illustration) from the green construction paper and glue them onto the plate next to the flowers.

Site:
Found in Thailand and other areas of tropical and subtropical Asia

⚙ **Floating Flowers.** Lotus flowers float on top of the water like a lily pad. Try floating your egg-carton lotus flowers in a tub of water. Blow on the flowers to move them around.
(Note: Adult supervision is *always* necessary around water — even if it's just a few inches/cm deep!)

⚙ **Name that Food!** In Asia, the roots of the lotus flower are often boiled or preserved in sugar. Its boiled leaves are eaten as a vegetable, and parts of the flower are made into tea. Can you think of foods that you eat that are made from roots, leaves, or flowers?

Indian Elephant

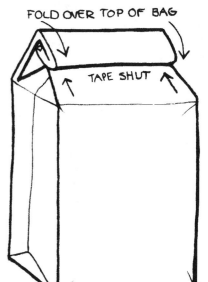

FOLD OVER TOP OF BAG

TAPE SHUT

What you need:

- Brown paper lunch bag
- Old newspapers
- Transparent tape
- Assorted markers
- Wiggly eyes (optional)
- Glue stick
- Brown and white construction paper
- Child safety scissors

Namastay!

Today was the Elephant Festival. The elephants' owners decorated their elephants and marched with them in a parade. The elephants walked very slowly. They are so wonderful and friendly. I love elephants!

Your Friend

What you do:

1. Loosely stuff the bag with crumpled newspapers. Fold over the top of the bag and tape flat.

2. Use a marker to draw the elephant's face onto the bag. Glue on the wiggly eyes.

3. Cut out the elephant's trunk and ears from the brown paper. Cut out the tusks from the white paper.

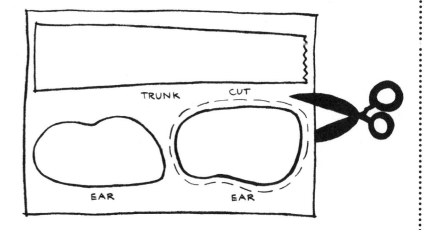

TRUNK   CUT

EAR   EAR

4. Use a marker to outline the ears and trunk. Glue the tusks, trunk, and ears onto the elephant.

AROUND the WORLD FUN!

⚙ **Try this Experiment.** Elephants are smart, hard workers! In India, elephants help workers lift and move logs. Put your hand inside an athletic sock. Practice lifting and moving things with your "trunk." How hard is it to pick up a box of cereal? A basketball? A toy car?

⚙ **Learn More!** Read *Big, Rough, and Wrinkly (What Am I?)* by Moira Butterfield and Wayne Ford.

Site:
Native to the Indian subcontinent and southeastern Asia. The African elephant is found in sub-Saharan Africa.

Flamingo

What you do:

1. Fold the pink paper and cut out both sides of the flamingo's body.

2. Twist a pipe cleaner for the flamingo's neck and head. Bend the other two cleaners for the legs. Tape the cleaners on one side of the flamingo's body. Tape the two body pieces together to cover the cleaners.

3. Use the marker to draw the flamingo's feathers.

Al salaam a'alaykum!
Today I saw flamingos, each standing on one leg. They eat by dipping their heads underwater. Then, they scoop backward with their heads upside down. What a funny way to take a drink of water!

Your Friend

What you need:

- Pink construction paper
- Child safety scissors
- 3 white pipe cleaners
- Transparent tape
- Pink marker

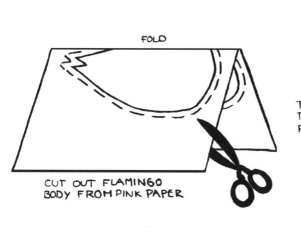

FOLD

CUT OUT FLAMINGO BODY FROM PINK PAPER

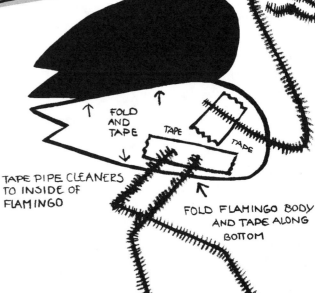

FOLD AND TAPE

TAPE

TAPE

TAPE PIPE CLEANERS TO INSIDE OF FLAMINGO

FOLD FLAMINGO BODY AND TAPE ALONG BOTTOM

Site:
Found in tropical
and subtropical
areas around the world.
The greater flamingo
(pale red) is found
in northwest India,
the Middle East,
the western
Mediterranean,
and Africa.
Other types
are found in
South America and
southeastern
North America.

☺ **Pretend Play.** Count the seconds you can stand on one leg like a flamingo. Practice and then play a game with your friends to see who can stand flamingo-style the longest.

☺ **Draw a Pink Picture.** When flamingos fly together, they look like a pink cloud in the sky. Use markers to draw a picture of flamingos in flight, a pink sunset, or silly pink elephants!

Orange Tree

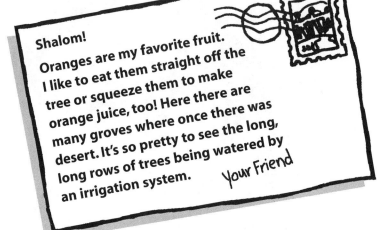

Shalom!

Oranges are my favorite fruit. I like to eat them straight off the tree or squeeze them to make orange juice, too! Here there are many groves where once there was desert. It's so pretty to see the long, long rows of trees being watered by an irrigation system.

Your Friend

What you do:

1. Wrap the tube in brown paper. Use the brown marker to draw on the bark for a tree trunk.

2. Fold the green paper in half and cut out two circles for the treetops. Cut out several circles from the orange paper for oranges.

What you need:

- Cardboard paper-towel tube
- Green, brown, and orange construction paper
- Brown and green markers
- Child safety scissors
- Transparent tape
- Glue stick

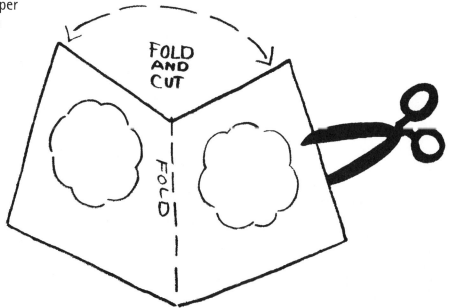

FOLD AND CUT

FOLD

TAPE BOTH SIDES TOGETHER

TAPE   TOGETHER

Site:
Jaffa orange tree found throughout Israel. Sweet and mandarin oranges are grown across the southern United States (in Florida, California, Texas, and Arizona) and in Brazil, China, Spain, Mexico, Italy, India, and Egypt.

3. Tape the two green circles together, with the trunk in the middle. Glue oranges onto the tree.

AROUND the WORLD FUN!

⚙ **Fruit Trees.** How many fruits can you name that grow on trees? On bushes? How about apples, pears, and figs?

⚙ **Plant a Desert Terrarium.** Fill a shallow, terra-cotta pot with planting soil. Plant cactus and other succulent plants. Sprinkle small pebbles over the surface of the soil. Place your terrarium in a sunny window and water sparingly.

Africa

Africa is the second largest continent (Asia, as you know, is the biggest). Africa is so exciting because there are deserts, mountains, beautiful rain forests, and wonderful animals there that don't live anywhere else in the world. Because Africa is divided into almost two equal parts by the equator, most of it is in the tropics, which means that it is very hot for most the year.

And guess what? Many people believe that the name *Africa* came from a very old Latin word meaning "sunny" or from a very old Greek word meaning "without cold." Because the sun shines so much there, nature has given the indigenous African people dark skin to help protect them from sunburn.

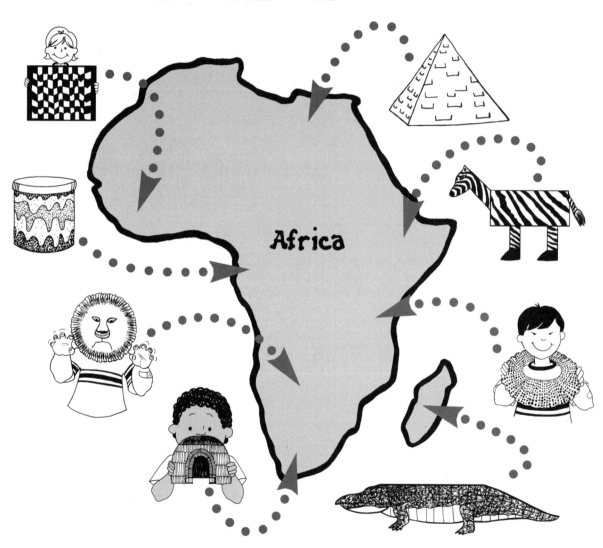

The Great Pyramid

Al salaam a'alaykum!

Today I visited the pyramids of ancient Egypt. Each pyramid is made from stone and has a square base with four triangles for sides. Great Egyptian kings from thousands of years ago, along with their families, pets, servants, and treasures, were buried in the pyramids. They are so huge — I wonder how they were built without heavy machines!

Your Friend

What you need:

- Cereal-box cardboard
- Pencil
- Child safety scissors
- Marker
- Ruler or straightedge
- Transparent tape

What you do:

1. Ask a grown-up to help you trace a 6" (15 cm) square onto the cardboard and cut out the square. Then, ask a grown-up to help you trace four 6" (15 cm) equilateral triangles (all three sides are equal) onto cardboard and cut them out.

TRACE SQUARE ONTO CARDBOARD

6" (15 CM)

CONTINUED...

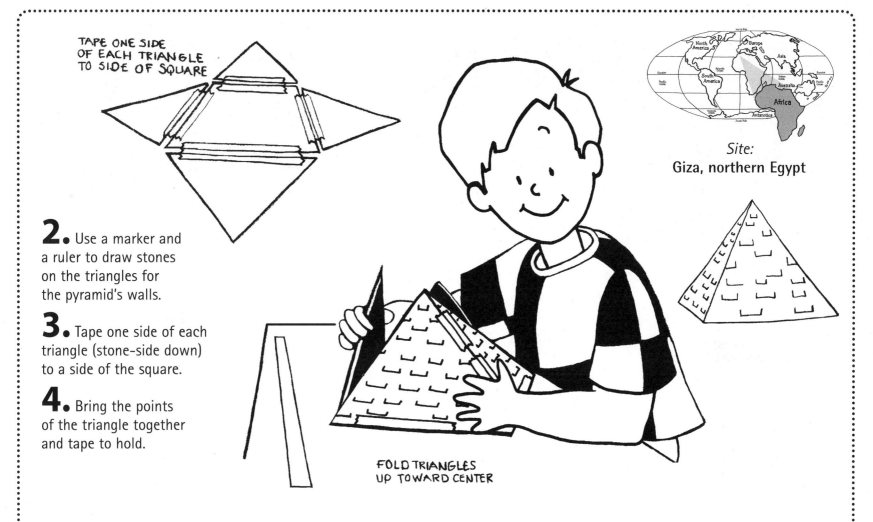

TAPE ONE SIDE OF EACH TRIANGLE TO SIDE OF SQUARE

Site:
Giza, northern Egypt

2. Use a marker and a ruler to draw stones on the triangles for the pyramid's walls.

3. Tape one side of each triangle (stone-side down) to a side of the square.

4. Bring the points of the triangle together and tape to hold.

FOLD TRIANGLES UP TOWARD CENTER

AROUND the WORLD FUN!

⚙ **King for a Day!** More than 3,000 years ago, *Tutankhamen* (too-tahn-KAH-mehn) became the king of Egypt when he was about 10 years old! Make yourself a crown with triangle shapes on a headband. If you were king, what rules would you make?

⚙ **Shapes!** Look around the room for things that are shaped like squares and triangles. How many can you see?

⚙ **Learn More!** To find out more about ancient Egypt and the pyramids, read the book *Mummies Made in Egypt* by Aliki.

Striped Zebra

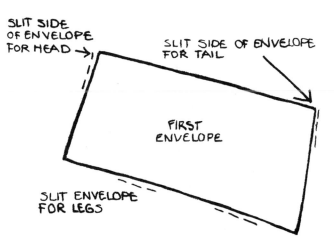

Selam!

Here's a riddle: What's black and white and "read" all over? Answer: a newspaper. A zebra is also black and white. If you look at a herd of zebras you can't tell them apart. Yet, no two zebras are alike when it comes to their stripes.

Your Friend

What you do:

1. Cut two slits along the bottom of one envelope. Cut a slit in both upper corners. Lick the flap closed.

2. Cut out the zebra's head and neck, legs, and tail from the second envelope.

What you need:

- 2 large white envelopes
- Child safety scissors
- Black construction paper
- Glue stick
- Black marker

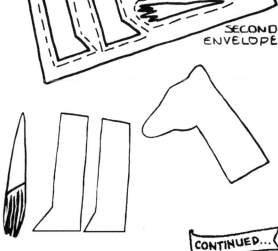

SLIT SIDE OF ENVELOPE FOR HEAD →

SLIT SIDE OF ENVELOPE FOR TAIL

FIRST ENVELOPE

SLIT ENVELOPE FOR LEGS

SECOND ENVELOPE

CONTINUED...

3. Tear thin strips of black paper and glue them diagonally across the envelope. Trim off any extra. Use a black marker to draw stripes on the zebra's head and neck, legs, and tail.

4. Glue the legs, tail, and head inside the slits in the envelope. Glue the openings closed.

TORN BLACK STRIPS

WHITE ENVELOPE

Site:
Arid, sparsely wooded areas in parts of Kenya, Ethiopia, and Somalia

AROUND the WORLD FUN!

⚙ **One of a Kind!** Pour a small amount of tempera paint onto a pad of moistened paper towels to make an ink pad. Press your fingertip into the pad and then onto paper. Compare your fingerprint with the fingerprints of your friends and family. Is each person's fingerprint different or the same?

⚙ **Learn More!** To discover more about zebras, read *The Zebra: Striped Horse* by Christine Denis-Huot.

Masai Beaded Necklace

Habari!
Today I met Masai men and women wearing wire jewelry. After they get married, Masai women wear many beaded collars. The jewelry is beautiful. It is very heavy. Believe it or not, this makes their necks grow very long!

Your Friend

What you need:

- Large paper plate
- Child safety scissors
- Assorted tempera paints, in dishes or lids
- Paintbrush

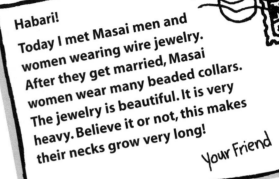

CUT CENTER OUT OF LARGE PAPER PLATE

CUT CENTER

What you do:

1. Cut into the plate and then cut out the center, leaving a wide rim all around.

2. Dip the rounded end of the paintbrush handle into a color. Press dots of color around the rim of the plate. Wash off the end of the paintbrush. Then, use another color for more dots.

CONTINUED...

AROUND the WORLD FUN!

⚙ **Beads Galore!** Purchase colorful beads and thin wires from a craft store. Thread the beads onto the wires for different bracelets and necklaces.

⚙ **Learn More!** Read the book *Growing Up Masai* by Tom Shactman to learn what life is like for Masai children.

Site:
North central Tanzania, southern Kenya

Nile Crocodile

What you need:

- Brown construction paper
- Pencil
- Child safety scissors
- Sponge (small piece)
- Green tempera paint, in a dish or lid
- Black marker

What you do:

1. Fold the paper in half the long way. With the fold at the top, draw a crocodile on the paper (see art on page 70 to trace).

2. Cut out the crocodile. (Make sure you do not cut the fold along the crocodile's back, though!)

DON'T CUT ON CROCODILE'S BACK

Hello!
Today I saw a big crocodile lying in the sun! It had its mouth open wide. When it closed its mouth, two of its lower teeth stuck out. The skin on the crocodile looks just like armor.

Your Friend

CONTINUED...

3. Dab the sponge in the paint. Press it onto the crocodile for skin. Use a marker to draw eyes and a mouth.

⚙ **Make a Crocodile Hand Puppet.** Put your hand inside an athletic sock. Push the toe of the sock into the curve of your hand between your thumb and pointer finger. Use fabric paint or a marker to draw on the crocodile's eyes. Now, move your fingers to open and close the crocodile's mouth!

⚙ **Crocodile Crafts!** To make more animal crafts, read *The Kids' Wildlife Book: Exploring Animal Worlds through Indoor/ Outdoor Crafts & Experiences* by Warner Shedd.

Site:
Found throughout tropical and southern Africa and Madagascar, in rivers, freshwater marshes, estuaries, and mangrove swamps

YOU CAN TRACE THIS ONTO YOUR FOLDED PAPER IN STEP 1.

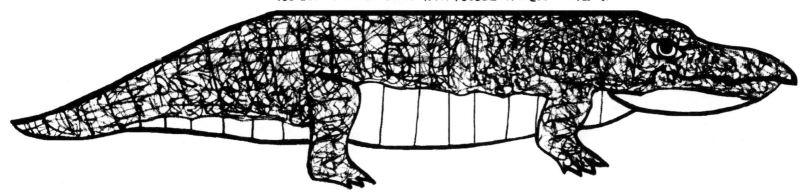

Lion Mask

What you need:

- Brown paper lunch bag
- Child safety scissors
- Pencil
- Large paper plate
- Glue stick
- Brown and black markers
- Yarn

What you do:

1. Cut open the paper bag and lay it flat. Ask a grown-up to help you trace the paper plate onto the bag. Cut out the circle slightly larger than the drawing.

Habari!

Today we went on a safari. I saw a beautiful lion! A lion is a cat, but it's not like my cat, Whiskers. Whiskers eats food from a can and curls up in my lap and purrs. Lions live on the open plains. They hunt for food and have a loud roar. I wouldn't want a lion to curl up in my lap!

Your Friend

CONTINUED...

2. Glue the circle onto the paper plate.

3. Cut out the lion's eyes. Cut along three sides of the nose as shown. Cut fringe around the lion's face for its mane.

4. Use a pencil to poke a hole in the sides of the plate. String yarn through the holes. Use the markers to decorate the face. Put on your mask and *r-o-a-r!*

Site:
Found mainly in parts of Africa south of the Sahara

CUT ALONG THREE SIDES OF NOSE

AROUND the WORLD FUN!

⚙ **A Proud Pride.**
Lions are the most social members of the cat family. They live in a group called a *pride*. Make several paper-plate lions to make a pride of lions.

⚙ **Learn More!** Read the book *Young Lions* by Toshi Yoshida to learn how lions in Africa hunt for food.

Zulu Beehive Hut

What you need:

- Brown paper lunch bag
- Child safety scissors
- Transparent tape
- Brown marker

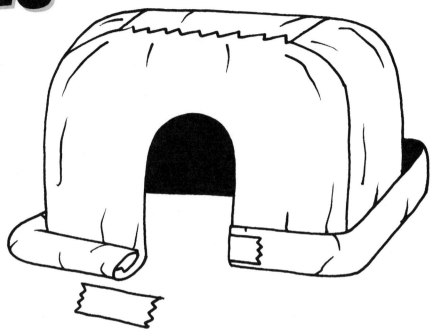

Hallo!

Today I saw beehive huts in a Zulu village. These huts are shaped like beehives and are covered with dry grass mats. The doorway to each hut is very small. You have to get on your hands and knees to crawl inside. I got to visit the nice people living inside one. It was fun!

Your Friend

What you do:

1. Cut away the top half of the bag. Hold the bottom of the bag upside down and cut out a doorway for a hut.

2. Fold up the edge of the bag for a cuff around the bottom of the hut. Tape at the corners as shown.

3. Use a marker to draw the grass mats on the hut. Push in the corners of the bag to round off the top of the hut.

CONTINUED...

Site:
**Kwazulu Natal,
southern Africa**

⚙ **Houses, Huts, and
Hives.** Beehive huts are
shaped like a beehive. They
have a dome-shaped roof.
Take a walk and look at
the roofs on the buildings
where you live. Describe
the roofs that you see.
Draw a picture of some
of the roof shapes.

⚙ **Not a Drop!** Zulu huts
in Africa are so well built
out of grasses that when
it rains, everyone inside
stays dry. How do you
stay dry on a rainy day?

Desert Sand Dune

What you need:

- Chalk, 3 or 4 colors
- Cheese grater
- Waxed paper
- Salt
- Small jar with a tight-fitting lid
- Thin paintbrush

What you do:

1. Grate each color of chalk over a sheet of waxed paper. Mix salt into the chalk.

2. Pour a layer of colored salt into the jar. Continue to add layers of different colors of salt. Fill the jar to the top.

Good morning!

I played in the sand today, but I wasn't at the beach. We were in the sand dunes in the desert. Sand dunes are always moving and changing. Wind blows grains of sand up and over the tops of the dunes and down the other side. Sand got in my shoes when I walked!

Your Friend

CONTINUED...

POKE END OF PAINT-
BRUSH INTO SALT
ALONG JAR TO
MAKE DESIGN

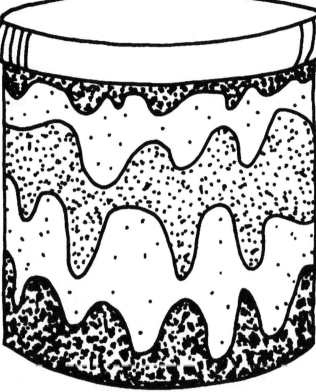

Site:
**Located in Africa
near the equator.
Other continents —
North America and
Asia, for instance —
have deserts, too.
Beach dunes can
be seen along many
coastal areas on
many continents.**

3. Poke the end of the
paintbrush into the salt along
the sides of the jar to make a
design. Tightly screw the lid
back onto the jar.

AROUND the WORLD FUN!

✿ **Paint with Sand.** Squeeze a design of white craft glue onto paper. Sprinkle different
colors of salt sand over the glue. Shake off the excess sand for a sand painting!

✿ **Beach in a Bag.** Each time you visit a beach, collect a small sandwich bag of sand. When
you get home, label the bag with the name of the beach and the date of your visit. How
does the sand from one beach compare with the sand from another beach?

Ashanti Kente Cloth

What you need:

- Assorted construction paper (3 sheets the same size, plus black)
- Child safety scissors
- Transparent tape

Greetings!

Today I saw some bright and colorful cloth, woven by Ashanti weavers. Strips of the cloth are sewn together. These kente cloths are worn during very special occasions — just like when I wear my best clothes.

Your Friend

What you do:

1. Fold the black paper in half. Starting at the fold, cut zigzag slits across the paper, stopping about 1" (2.5 cm) from the edge. Lay the paper flat.

FOLD OVER

CONTINUED...

2. Cut assorted colors of paper into strips. Weave strips of paper in and out of the slits — first *over* one slit, then *under* the next slit, through to the other side. Tape the ends of the strips to keep them in place.

3. Weave the next strip, starting *under* the slit, then going *over*. Alternate each strip until the black paper is completely woven.

TAPE

← TAPE THE ENDS TO KEEP IN PLACE.

Site:
Made in parts of Ghana and Cote d'Ivoire

AROUND the WORLD FUN!

✿ **Weaving Leaves.** Pull out several threads from a piece of burlap fabric. Weave a collection of dried leaves, weeds, and twigs through the openings in the fabric. Hang the burlap from yarn tied to a stick.

✿ **Coats of Many Colors.** Think about the clothes you wear on special occasions, like family dinners, birthday parties, and playtime. Think about the kinds of clothes you wear at different times of the year. How are winter and summer clothes different? How do you think African clothes might differ from your clothes?

Europe

Europe is one of the world's smaller continents. (Asia is four times as big!) And guess what? The smallest country in the world is in Europe. (It's the Vatican City.) You already may have heard of some of the countries in Europe, such as *France*, *England*, and *Spain*. Europe has many other countries, too, and in each one, people speak a different language. Yet, all of the people who live in Europe are called Europeans.

Even though there are many countries on this continent, the countries are all very near to one another — as near as you may be to another state or province. Imagine: Some people who live in France drive to the store in *Germany* or buy their clothes in *Switzerland!* How would you like to be able to visit another country just by hopping in your family's car and driving down the road? That would be so much fun!

Clicking Castanet

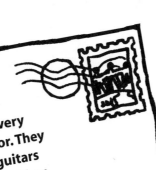

¡Hola!
We watched *flamenco* dancers click their heels very quickly on the dance floor. They danced to the music of guitars and chattering castanets. When they finished their dance, we all clapped and yelled, "Olé!"

Your Friend

What you need:

- Cereal-box cardboard
- Child safety scissors
- 2 large buttons*
- Tacky glue
- Markers

Buttons pose a choking danger to young children. Adults should control the supply and insert them into the project.

What you do:

1. Cut out the shape as shown from the cardboard.

2. Glue a button on each end for castanets. Allow to dry.

3. Use markers to decorate the castanets. Fold over.

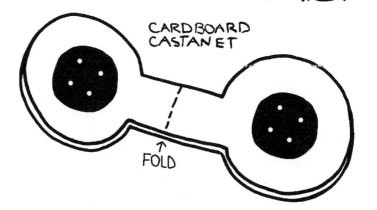

CARDBOARD CASTANET

FOLD

AROUND the WORLD FUN!

⚙ **Be a Spanish Dancer!** A woman flamenco dancer wears a lace *mantilla* over her head and shoulders. Ask a grown-up to help attach a scarf to your hair using barrettes. Now, hold your hands high, click your castanets and your heels, and dance!

⚙ **Play the Spoons.** Clap together two metal spoons. Hold one spoon between your thumb and index finger with the spoon facing up. Hold the second spoon, bottom facing up, between your third and fourth fingers. To play the spoons, sit down and click the spoons between your thigh and the palm of your other hand.

Site: Used specifically in Spain, but also wherever there are flamenco dancers. Variations can be found throughout Eastern Europe into Asia.

Eiffel Tower

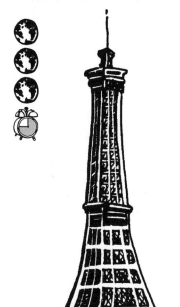

What you need:

- Construction paper (3 sheets)
- Transparent tape
- Child safety scissors
- Pencil
- Sharp scissors (for grown-up use only)
- Black marker

What you do:

1. Fold one sheet of construction paper in half the long way. Open it, lay it flat, and fold each long side to the center crease. Tape the long sides together to make a long rectangular tube.

Bonjour!

I took an elevator to the top of the Eiffel Tower this evening. When I got to the top I looked out over the city. I could see all of Paris. What a beautiful sight! Now I know why it's called the "City of Lights!"

Your Friend

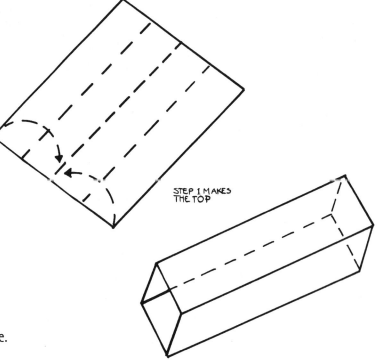

STEP 1 MAKES THE TOP

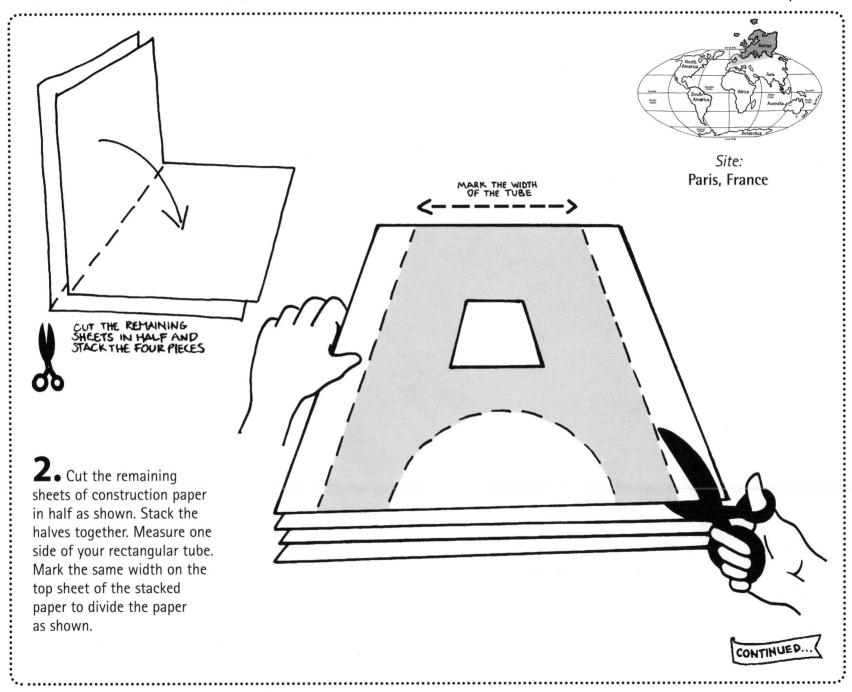

CUT THE REMAINING SHEETS IN HALF AND STACK THE FOUR PIECES

MARK THE WIDTH OF THE TUBE

Site:
Paris, France

2. Cut the remaining sheets of construction paper in half as shown. Stack the halves together. Measure one side of your rectangular tube. Mark the same width on the top sheet of the stacked paper to divide the paper as shown.

CONTINUED...

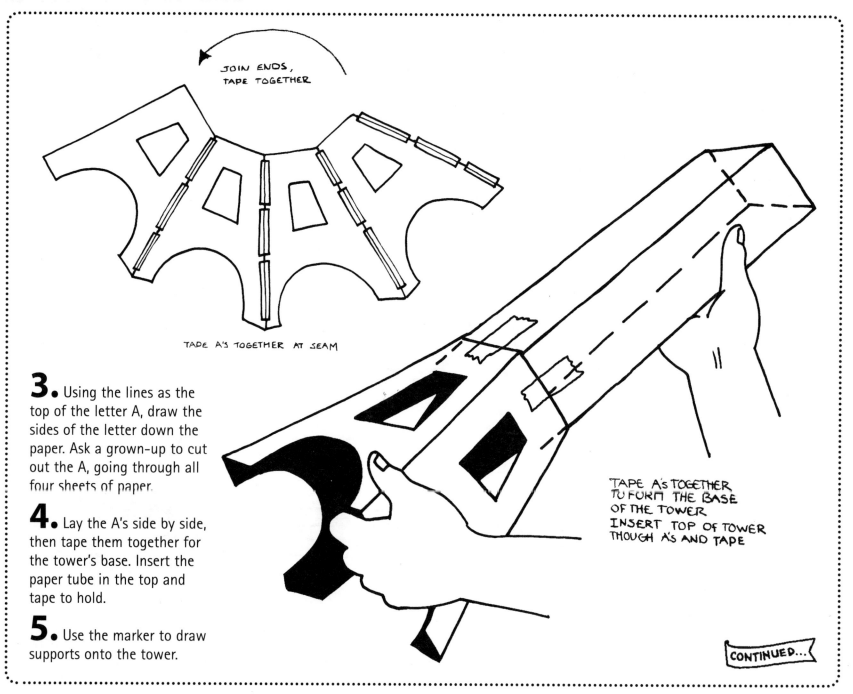

JOIN ENDS, TAPE TOGETHER

TAPE A's TOGETHER AT SEAM

3. Using the lines as the top of the letter A, draw the sides of the letter down the paper. Ask a grown-up to cut out the A, going through all four sheets of paper.

4. Lay the A's side by side, then tape them together for the tower's base. Insert the paper tube in the top and tape to hold.

5. Use the marker to draw supports onto the tower.

TAPE A's TOGETHER TO FORM THE BASE OF THE TOWER INSERT TOP OF TOWER THOUGH A's AND TAPE

CONTINUED...

The Nose Knows.
Locally grown flowers such as wild lavender, jasmine, and violets are used to create French perfumes. Smell the flowers that grow where you live. Ask a florist or gardener if you could have some flowers that have gone by. Place the petals in a bowl. Do they make your room smell nice?

Story Corner.
Read the timeless and enchanting *The Adventures of Jeanne-Marie* by Françoise.

Decorated Egg

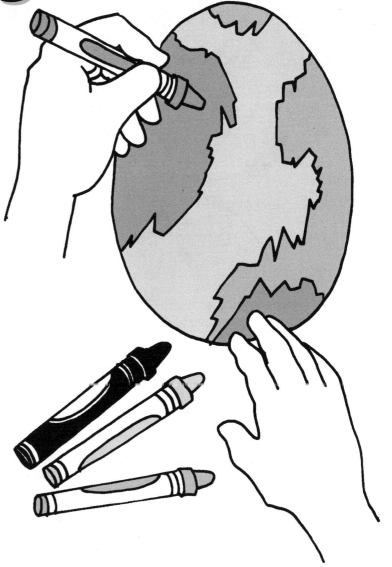

Nazdar!

In the marketplace this morning I saw beautifully decorated eggs. These eggs are called *pysanky*. Each egg has a different design. The designs are made with wax and dye. They're too beautiful to eat!

Your Friend

What you need:

- Small white paper plate
- Child safety scissors
- Crayons (including black)
- Pencil with a dull point or toothpicks

What you do:

1. Cut out the shape of an egg from the center of the paper plate.

2. Use colorful crayons to cover the egg with blotches of color.

3. Color heavily over the whole egg with a black crayon.

4. Use the pencil to scratch designs in the egg.

Around the World Fun!

Site:
A popular craft in Eastern Europe and many parts of Russia

⚙ **Eggs-traordinary!** Very gently draw designs on the shell of a raw egg using a white crayon or a wax candle Hold the egg over a bowl. Ask a grown-up to poke a very small hole in each end. Use a straw to blow the contents of the egg into the bowl.* Carefully wash the egg in soap and water. Dip it into a cup of water mixed with a few drops of food coloring. Remove the egg and let it dry. The food coloring won't stick to the wax design, so you'll have a pysanky-style egg!

⚙ **Egyptian Egg Art.** Lots of countries make colored eggs to celebrate the spring. Ask a grown-up to help you cut out an egg shape from cardboard. Fill a cup with water and a few drops of food coloring. Break eggshells into small pieces* and place them in the food coloring. Strain the shells when colored and pat them dry with paper towels. Cover the cardboard with glue and press on the colored eggshell pieces.

*Save the eggs' insides to make breakfast!

Matryoshka

What you need:

- Assorted construction paper
- Child safety scissors
- Transparent tape
- Markers

Strozveetsya!

Big, bigger, biggest. These nesting dolls fit inside each other! Just when you think you've uncovered the smallest doll, there's one that's even smaller. When they're standing in a row, they look like a doll family!

Your Friend

What you do:

1. Cut out half circles, going from large to small, from different colors of construction paper. Bend in and tape the corners together.

2. Cut out faces from construction paper, going from large to small. Use markers to draw eyes, nose, mouth, and hair on each face.

3. Tape the faces inside the taped half circles. Stack the dolls, starting with the smallest and ending with the largest.

BEND ENDS

TAPE

TAPE ENDS TOGETHER

Site:
Most popular in Russia, though they can be found in Eastern Europe as well

⚙ **Around-the-World Names.** *Matryoshka* means "a little Matryona." *Matryona* is the Russian word for "mother." Do you have a nickname? Ask your friends and family what they like to be called.

⚙ **Size Things Up.** Arrange things like cans, boxes, toy cars, or stuffed animals according to size. Start with the biggest and move to the smallest. Then, reverse the order.

Castle

Guten tag!

We saw many castles when we went for a boat ride down the Rhine River yesterday. Castles were built as forts so that the owners could protect their lands and their families. Imagine living in a house that big!

Your Friend

What you need:

- Cereal-box cardboard
- Sharp scissors (for grown-up use only)
- Construction paper (one color plus black and a scrap of red)
- Transparent tape
- 2 cardboard toilet-paper tubes
- Tacky glue
- Child safety scissors
- Black marker

What you do:

1. Ask a grown-up to cut the cereal box in half. Wrap the top half of the box in construction paper and tape to hold.

2. Wrap the cardboard tubes in construction paper. Glue a tube to each side of the cereal box.

3. Cut out a 6" (15 cm) circle from the black paper. Make a single cut from the outside edge of the circle into the center. Overlap the edges and tape them together to form a peaked turret. Glue a roof on top of each tube.

4. Use the marker to draw stones, windows, and a doorway on the castle. Cut two flags from the red paper and glue one onto each turret.

CUT HORIZONTALLY

MAKE A CUT TO CENTER OF CIRCLE. FOLD AND OVERLAP TO FORM CASTLE PEAK. TAPE TOGETHER.

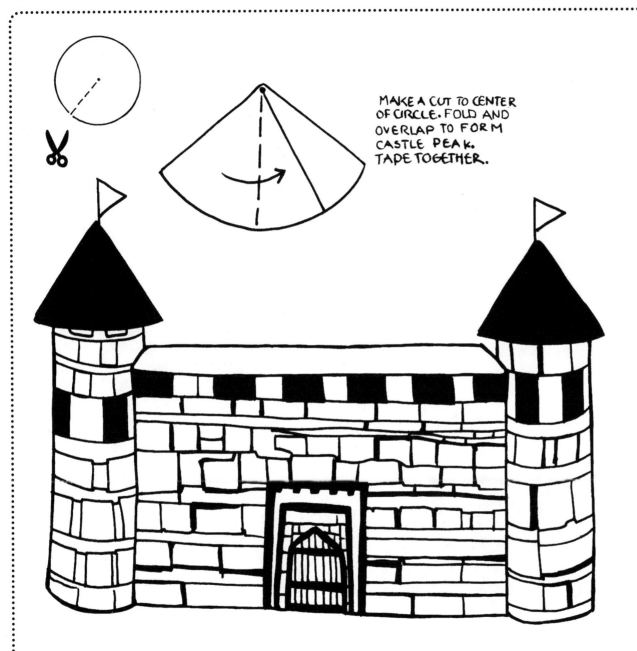

Site:
Found throughout Europe, with many of the best-preserved examples in Germany

AROUND the WORLD FUN!

✪ **Build a Castle.** Use things found in your kitchen cupboard. How about tin cans for towers and cardboard boxes for walls? What will you put inside your castle? How about small dolls, action figures, and animals?

✪ **Story Corner.** Look at the book *Into the Castle* by June Crebbin.

The Little Mermaid

What you do:

1. Cut out a picture of a person from an old magazine or photo (maybe one of you!). Cut away the legs in the picture.

2. Cut out fins from the green construction paper. Glue the fins onto the picture to make a mermaid.

3. Glue the mermaid onto the Popsicle stick. Cut a slit in the bottom of the cup, then push the Popsicle stick down into the slit.

What you need:

- Old magazine or photo
- Child safety scissors
- Green construction paper
- Glue stick
- Popsicle stick
- Paper cup

Davs!

This afternoon I saw the Little Mermaid, a statue that sits in the harbor in Copenhagen. She's supposed to be half-human and half-fish. This mermaid is sitting on a rock looking out to sea. I wonder what she is thinking about.

Your Friend

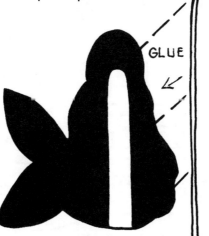

GLUE

GLUE BACK OF MERMAID TO POPSICLE STICK

CUT A SLIT IN BOTTOM OF CUP FOR STICK

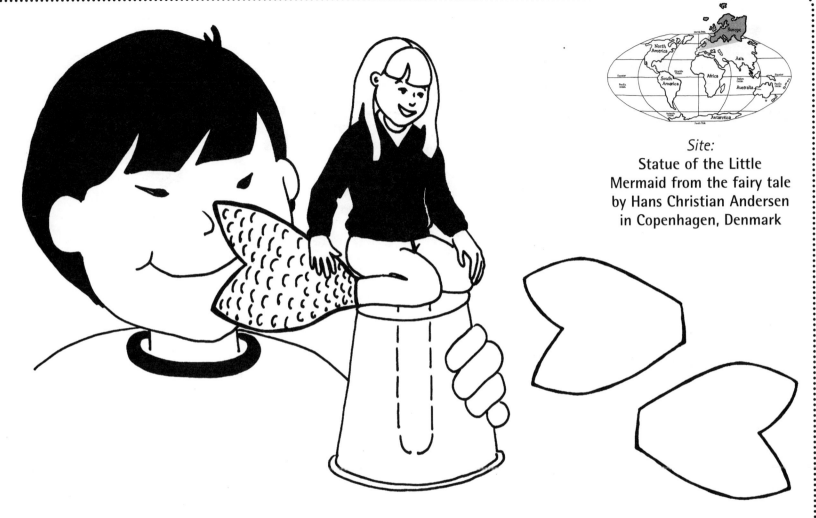

Site:
Statue of the Little Mermaid from the fairy tale by Hans Christian Andersen in Copenhagen, Denmark

AROUND the WORLD FUN!

✿ **Mythical Animal Match.** Draw or paint pictures of pretend animals like unicorns, mermaids, and dragons onto index cards. Cut the index cards in half. Turn the cards face-down. The first player turns two cards over. If the halves match, that player keeps the cards. If not, the player turns the cards back over and it's the next player's turn. Take turns until there are no cards left.

✿ **Story Corner.** Read the book *The Mermaid Lullaby* by Kate Spohn.

Windmill

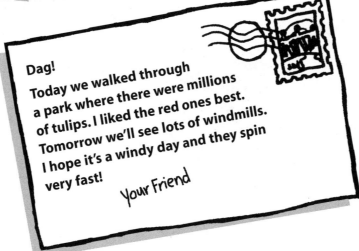

> Dag!
> Today we walked through a park where there were millions of tulips. I liked the red ones best. Tomorrow we'll see lots of windmills. I hope it's a windy day and they spin very fast!
>
> Your Friend

What you need:

- Round cardboard carton with lid (oatmeal, cornmeal, or bread-crumb container)
- Assorted construction paper
- Transparent tape
- Child safety scissors
- Black marker
- Sharp pointed tool (for grown-up use only)
- Paper fastener*

Paper fasteners pose a choking and poking danger to young children. Adults should control the supply and help insert them into the project.

AROUND the WORLD FUN!

✿ **Tide's In!** In Holland, the land is very low, and the sea is very high. *Dikes* are strong walls that hold back the sea. If you go to the beach, build a sand dike (wall) close to the shoreline. What happens to your dike when the tide comes in?

✿ **Bulb Magic.** Tulips grow all over Holland. These flowers grow from *bulbs*. Did you know that we eat some bulbs, such as beets, onions, and garlic? Put an onion in a brown bag. Wait a week or two, then look inside to see what is growing. Surprise!

✿ **Story Corner.** Read the book *The Hole in the Dike* retold by Norma Green and illustrated by Eric Carle.

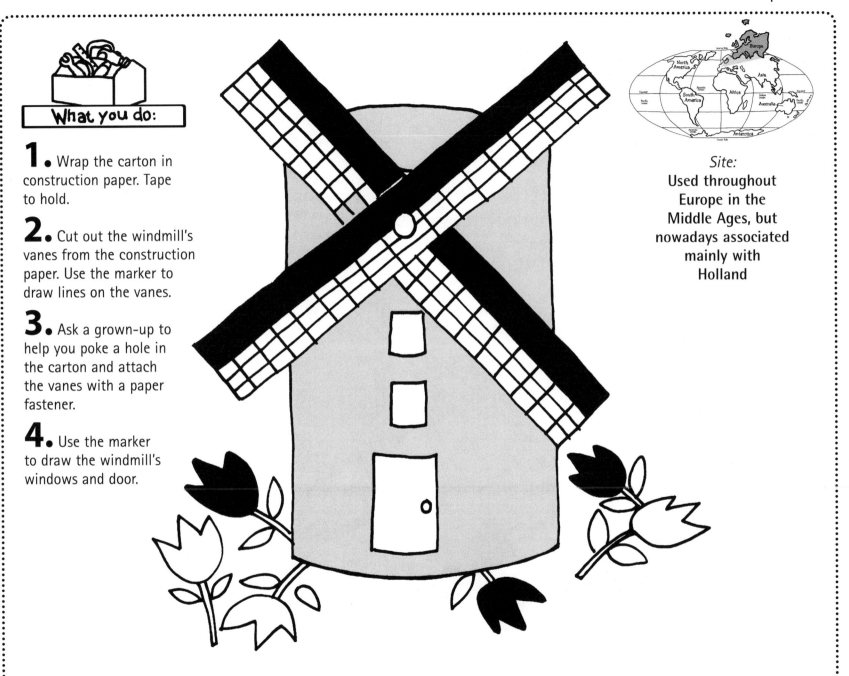

What you do:

1. Wrap the carton in construction paper. Tape to hold.

2. Cut out the windmill's vanes from the construction paper. Use the marker to draw lines on the vanes.

3. Ask a grown-up to help you poke a hole in the carton and attach the vanes with a paper fastener.

4. Use the marker to draw the windmill's windows and door.

Site:
Used throughout Europe in the Middle Ages, but nowadays associated mainly with Holland

Royal Crown

What you need:

- Cereal-box cardboard
- Ruler
- Child safety scissors
- Aluminum foil
- Transparent tape
- Cotton balls
- White craft glue
- Markers

What you do:

1. Cut out a 3" (8 cm) strip from cardboard. Measure the cardboard strip around your head and trim it to fit.

2. Cut a zigzag pattern down one side of the cardboard to make points on the crown.

3. Cover the cardboard in foil. Tape the ends together for a crown.

4. Glue cotton balls around the base of the crown. Use markers to decorate the crown. Let dry.

Good day!

If I were king or queen, I would invite my friends over and let them take turns wearing my crown. Today I saw the real crown jewels that the kings and queens of England have worn throughout history. You should see all the jewels! I think those crowns must be heavy to wear.

Your Friend

MEASURE AND CUT CARDBOARD

"Crackers"! No, these aren't the kind you eat with peanut butter. These are English party favors. To make a cracker, fill a cardboard toilet-paper tube with sweets and small toys. Wrap the tube in gift-wrap paper that's twice as long as the tube. Twist the ends of the paper and tie them with ribbon or yarn. Then, have a royal English party and wear your crown!

A Royal Website!
To see photos of the real crown jewels of England, check out this website: **www.camelot-group.com/tower_site/jewels/index.html**

Site:
British crown jewels on display in the Tower of London, London, England

Loch Ness Monster

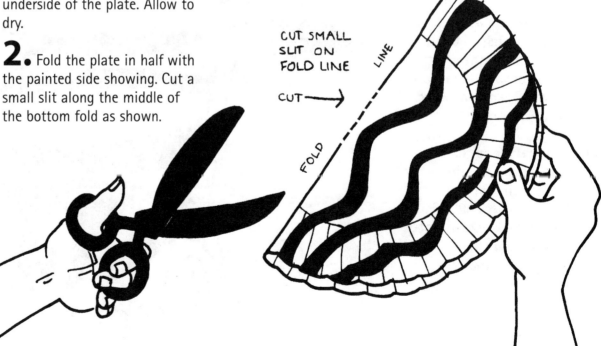

Ciamar a tha thu?

Legend has it that there's a shy monster called "Nessie" living in the Loch Ness. We went for a boat ride on the lake. I looked for the monster but didn't see it.

Your Friend

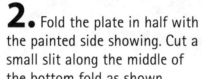

What you do:

1. Use the paints to color the underside of the plate. Allow to dry.

2. Fold the plate in half with the painted side showing. Cut a small slit along the middle of the bottom fold as shown.

CUT SMALL SLIT ON FOLD LINE

LINE

CUT ⟶

FOLD

What you need:

- Blue and green watercolor paints
- Paintbrush
- Small white paper plate
- Child safety scissors
- Green construction paper
- Black marker
- Popsicle stick
- Glue stick

3. Cut out the Loch Ness monster from the green paper. Use the marker to draw on the monster's face. Glue the monster onto the stick.

4. Insert the stick through the slit in the plate. Glue the corners of the plate together. Now, move the stick to move the monster!

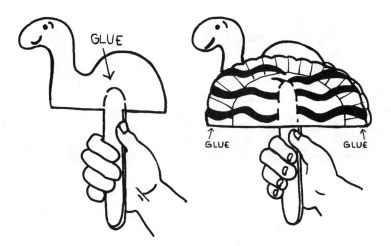

Site:
Loch Ness, Scotland

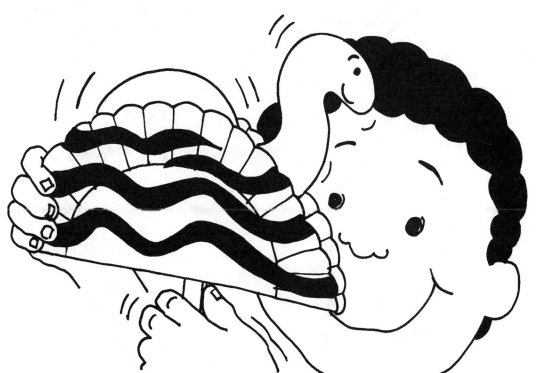

⚙ **Family Fabrics.** In the Scottish highlands, people wear special plaid clothing with a certain pattern and color that is their "family" cloth. Use markers to make up a plaid pattern on paper for your family.

⚙ **Monster Madness!** Everyone loves Nessie. Did you know she even has a fan club? Visit the club's website at: **www. lochness.co.uk/fan_ club/index.html**

Central and South America

This continent was named for the European explorer *Amerigo Vespucci* — just like North America was. Actually, the name "America" first meant only South America. Later, all three areas became known as the Americas.

Except for Antarctica, South America goes farther south than any other continent. And like Antarctica, it has some very cold spots, especially the Andes Mountains, which run almost all the way up the western side of the continent.

Other parts of this continent have beautiful rain forests with wonderful animals and plants that you can see only there. It will be so much fun to walk through a rain forest, seeing all of the strange, colorful birds and listening to the unusual sounds they make! I'd better bring an umbrella in case it starts to rain!

Central America

South America

Worry Doll

What you need:

- 1 ½ pipe cleaners
- Child safety scissors
- Scrap construction paper
- Markers
- Tacky glue
- Yarn
- Scrap fabric (small pieces)

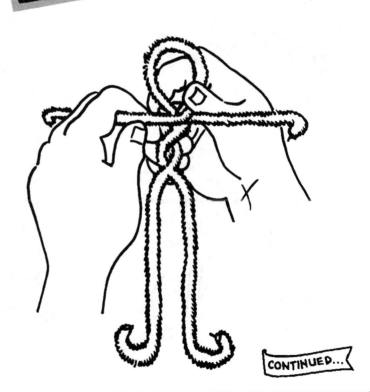

¡Hola!

Tonight I'll put a worry doll under my pillow just like the kids in Central America do. Before I fall asleep, I can tell it all my worries. In the morning when I wake up, my worries will be gone! That's what the tradition of the worry doll says.

Your Friend

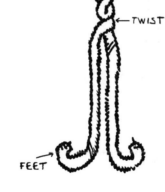

LOOP

← TWIST

FEET →

What you do:

1. Bend the whole pipe cleaner in half so a loop forms in the top. Twist the loop to make the doll's head. Bend the ends of the cleaner for the doll's feet.

2. Wrap the half-cleaner around the bottom of the loop for arms.

CONTINUED...

3. Cut out the doll's face from scrap paper. Use markers to draw on the doll's eyes, nose, mouth, and ears. Glue the face onto the loop. Glue on yarn for hair.

4. Wrap scrap fabric around the doll and glue to hold.

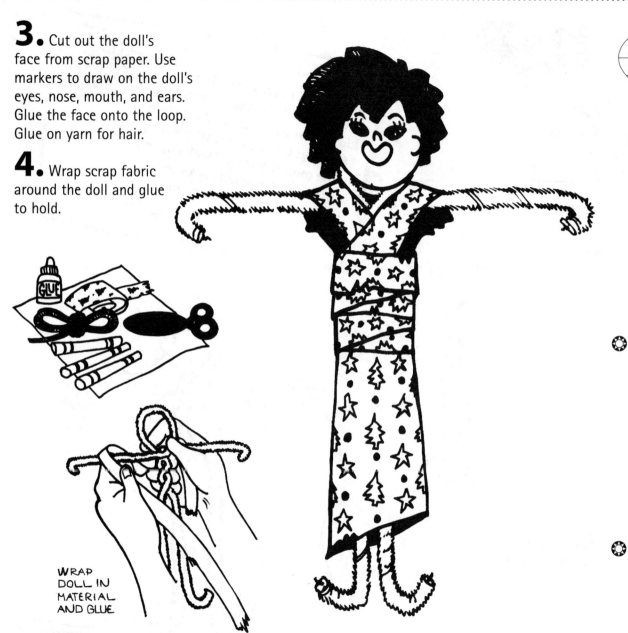

WRAP DOLL IN MATERIAL AND GLUE

Site:
Guatemala and parts of Mexico

AROUND the WORLD FUN!

✺ **Make a Doll Family.** Dolls of all different sizes can be found in the open-air markets of Central America. Try making a smaller worry doll. How small a piece of pipe cleaner will you need? Have fun making a whole family of dolls — and make some to give to friends, too.

✺ **Bejeweled!** Attach a small pipe cleaner loop around a small worry doll and through a ponytail holder, safety pin, or barrette for a great piece of craft jewelry.

Musical Maraca

What you need:

- Yogurt cup
- Seeds or beans
- Clear plastic wrap
- Rubber band
- Child safety scissors
- Brown paper lunch bag
- Transparent tape
- Markers

¡Hola!

I like the rattling sound of the shaking maraca. Maracas used to be made from dried gourd shells that had seeds inside. The maraca I played was made from wood. It was fun to hold a maraca in each hand and play along with songs I heard!

Your Friend

What you do:

1. Fill the empty cup with dried beans or seeds. Cover the opening with plastic wrap and secure with the rubber band.

2. Cut open the paper bag and lay it flat. Wrap the cup inside. Tape to hold.

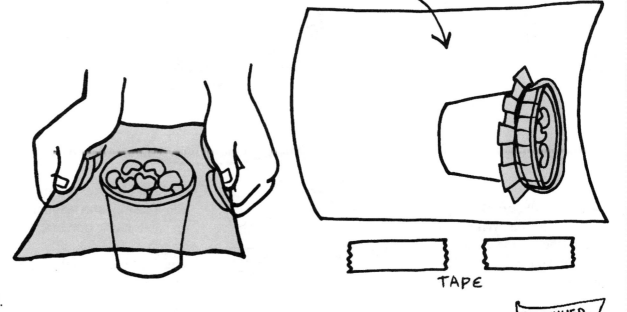

WRAP CUP IN PAPER BAG
TAPE TO HOLD

TAPE

CONTINUED...

Site:
Gourd maracas are very common in Venezuela, although variations of this instrument can be found all over the world.

3. Twist the excess bag to form a handle. Wrap tape around the handle. Now, decorate your maraca with markers and give it a shake!

AROUND the WORLD FUN!

⚙ **Maraca Madness!** Gather some maracas, a block of wood and a spoon, and a spoon and a pot lid. Have a parade. Put on some music and march around!

⚙ **Learn More!** To find out more about other percussion instruments from around the world, read *Bang and Rattle* by Ruth Thomson and Sally Hewitt or *Wood-Hoopoe Willie* by Katherine Roundtree and Virginia L. Kroll.

Gold Mask

What you need:

- Large paper plate
- Child safety scissors
- Pencil
- Yarn
- Aluminum foil
- Glue stick
- Yellow or orange marker

What you do:

1. Cut away the bottom third of the paper plate. On the remaining piece, draw eyes and a nose. Cut out the eyes. Cut along three sides of the nose as shown.

¡Hola!

I'm visiting ancient ruins and guess what I saw — gold! The early people of Colombia mined gold from rivers and mountains. They believed that gold was the "sweat of the sun." They made golden masks, statues, animal figures, drinking cups, and even a tiny gold raft. Just imagine how beautiful they all are!

Your Friend

CONTINUED...

2. Use a pencil to poke a hole on opposite sides of the plate. Thread yarn through each hole.

3. Glue pieces of aluminum foil onto the plate until the mask is covered. Use a marker to color it "gold." Let dry.

Site:
Found in The Gold Museum in Santafé de Bogotá, Colombia, although gold masks were also cast in ancient Egypt

GLUE ON FOIL AND THEN COLOR WITH MARKER

AROUND the WORLD FUN!

⚙ **Have a Treasure Hunt.** Gather several small rocks. Paint them gold. Hide the rocks around your house or yard. At the word "Go," players hunt for the rocks.

⚙ **Celebrate!** Just think how much fun it would be to wear your mask in an Indian or Spanish carnival or parade. To find out about celebrations, read *Hands Around the World* by Susan Milord.

Giant Tortoise

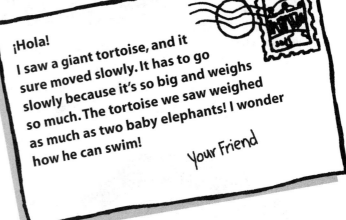

¡Hola!
I saw a giant tortoise, and it sure moved slowly. It has to go slowly because it's so big and weighs so much. The tortoise we saw weighed as much as two baby elephants! I wonder how he can swim!

Your Friend

What you need:

- Brown paper grocery bag
- Child safety scissors
- Transparent tape
- Brown marker

What you do:

1. Cut open the bag so it lays flat. Cut out a large oval from the bag.

2. Cut a slit in both ends of the oval. Overlap the ends of each slit and tape each to hold for the tortoise's curved shell.

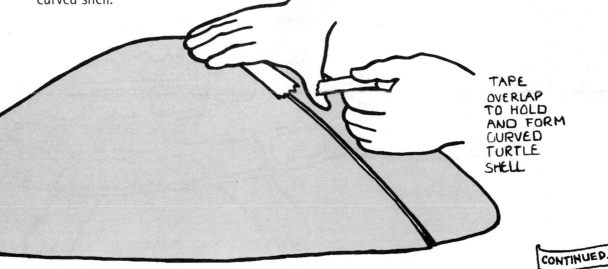

TAPE OVERLAP TO HOLD AND FORM CURVED TURTLE SHELL

CONTINUED...

3. Cut out the tortoise's head, tail, and feet from the rest of the bag. Tape to the underside of the shell. Use the marker to draw a pattern onto the tortoise's shell.

AROUND the WORLD FUN!

✪ **Story Corner.** Read the wonderful tale of *The Foolish Tortoise* by Richard Buckley.

✪ **Learn More!** Giant tortoises are *endangered* animals. That means we need to make sure their babies, called *tortoise hatchlings*, are able to grow up. Read the book *Gone Forever!* by Sandra and William Markele to learn more about endangered animals.

Site:
Most islands in the Galápagos Islands in the east Pacific off the coast of Ecuador

Emerald Tree Boa Constrictor

¡Hola!

Walking through a jungle, I saw a bright green boa constrictor in a tree above me. It stayed in the tree by wrapping itself around a thick branch. Up in the trees it finds monkeys and birds to eat. I'm glad I'm on the ground!

Your Friend

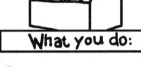

What you need:

- Green construction paper
- Transparent tape
- Child safety scissors
- Sponge (small piece)
- White tempera paint, in a dish or lid
- Black marker

What you do:

1. Roll the green paper into a long, thin tube. Tape to hold.

2. Cut around the ends of the tube for the snake's tail and head.

ROLL GREEN PAPER INTO TUBE.

TAPE TO HOLD

CUT AROUND ENDS TO FORM TAIL AND HEAD

CONTINUED...

3. Starting below the head, cut slits about 1" (2.5 cm) apart, being careful not to cut all the way through the tube.

4. Dab the sponge into the paint. Press it onto the tube for the snake's skin. Use the marker to draw the snake's eyes and mouth.

Site:
tropical South America

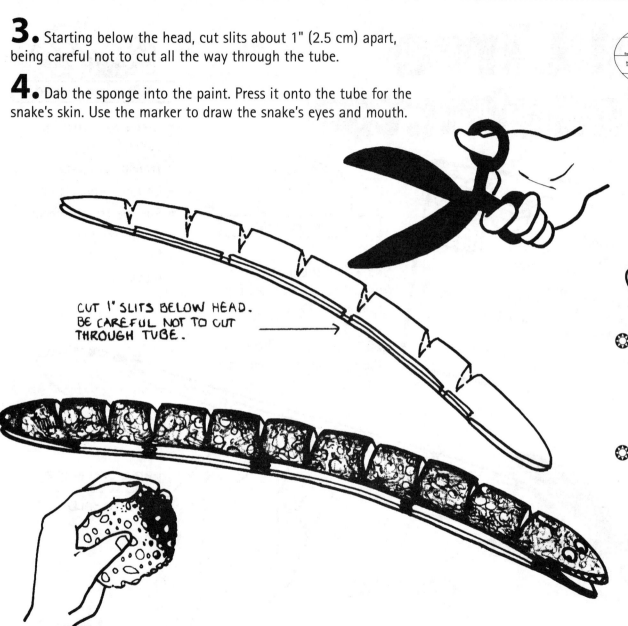

CUT 1" SLITS BELOW HEAD.
BE CAREFUL NOT TO CUT
THROUGH TUBE.

⚙ **Hometown Habitat.** Do you see squirrels, birds, or rabbits where you live? Draw a picture of the wildlife near your home.

⚙ **Take a "Smell Test"!** A snake smells with its tongue, as well as its nose. Try taking a "smell test." Gather things that have strong smells, like onions, lemons, pickles, coffee, and flowers. Put on a blindfold and see how many things you can identify just by their smell.

Carved Stone Statue

What you need:

- 2 brown paper lunch bags
- Old newspapers
- Brown marker
- Child safety scissors

What you do:

1. Loosely stuff the first bag with crumpled newspapers.

2. Hold the second bag upside down and draw on the statue's face with the brown marker.

3. Cut around three sides of the nose as shown.

CONTINUED...

4. Place the second bag over the stuffed bag for a 3-D statue.

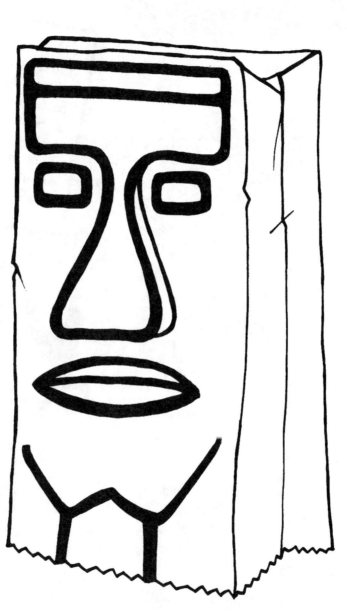

Site:
Easter Island, Chile

⚙ **Create a Story.** Imagine you came across stone statues with sad faces. What would you think those statues were sad about and why would the carvers have made them so sad? Make up a story to explain the "mystery behind the stone statues."

⚙ **Mysterious Places!** To see photos of the real Easter Island statues, check out this website: **www.mysterious-places.com/**

Gaucho Belt

What you need:

- Cereal-box cardboard
- Child safety scissors
- Pencil
- Aluminum foil
- Transparent tape
- Yarn
- Plastic straws

¡Hola!

We rode on horseback today, just like the gauchos! Gauchos rode the *pampas* (plains) on horseback, much like the cowboys of the old West did! They tamed wild horses and herded cattle. Gauchos wore thick leather belts decorated with silver and sometimes with old coins.

Your Friend

What you do:

1. Cut an oval shape from the cardboard. Use a pencil to poke a hole in each end. Cover the oval with foil and tape to hold.

CONTINUED...

2. Measure the yarn to fit around your waist, with some extra for tying. Then, cut the whole length in half. Tie one end of each half through a hole in the oval buckle.

3. Cut the straws into 2" (5 cm) lengths. Thread the pieces onto the yarn ties. Knot the yarn after the last straw on each side. Now, put on your gaucho belt!

MEASURE YARN TO FIT AROUND YOUR WAIST AND CUT

Site:
Argentina

AROUND the WORLD FUN!

✪ **Jazz it Up!** Here's a way to decorate the silver buckle on your gaucho belt. Before adding the foil, glue some string in a decorative pattern onto the cardboard. Allow the glue to dry. Then, wrap the cardboard in foil. Gently press over the foil to reveal the string design.

✪ **Story Corner.** Read *The Magic Bean Tree: A Legend from Argentina* by Nancy Van Laan.

Reco-Reco

What you need:

- Corrugated cardboard
- Sharp scissors (for grown-up use only)
- Unsharpened pencil

Olá!

I played a South American instrument today. The reco-reco is a scraper type of instrument. You scrape the stick along the strings to make a great sound. It is a percussion instrument like bells, drums, cymbals, and the triangle. I'd like to take reco-reco lessons when we get home so I can play in a band.

Your Friend

What you do:

1. Ask a grown-up to help you cut out a fancy shape from the cardboard.

2. Peel back the top layer of the cardboard to reveal the ribs.

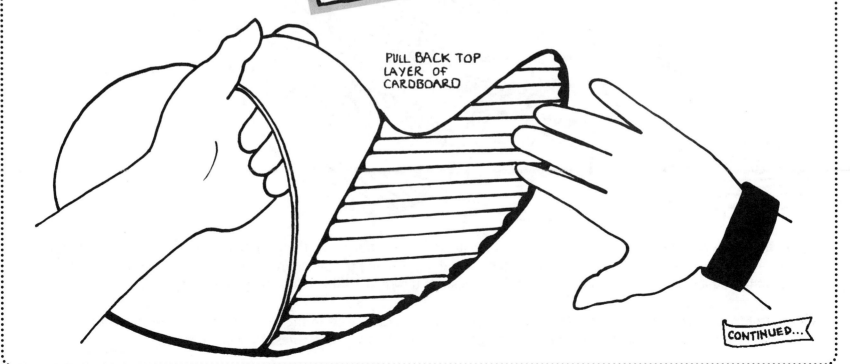

PULL BACK TOP LAYER OF CARDBOARD

CONTINUED...

3. Scrape the pencil across the ribs to create sounds.

Site:
Brazil

AROUND the WORLD FUN!

⚙ **Instruments Everywhere!** In ancient times, people made instruments out of things they found. Look for things around your house and outdoors that will make a scraping sound. Try running the pencil over the trunk of a tree, a concrete sidewalk, and a cheese grater. Listen to the different sounds they make. Which do you like the best?

⚙ **Learn More!** Brazil is home to the Amazon River, one of the greatest rivers in the world. To learn more about life in the forests of the Amazon, read *The Great Kapok Tree: A Tale of the Amazon Rain Forest* by Lynne Cherry.

Giant Armadillo

What you need:

- 2 small paper plates
- Child safety scissors
- Cereal-box cardboard
- Transparent tape
- Brown tempera paint, in a dish or lid
- Black marker

¡Hola!
I scared an armadillo today, but I didn't mean to! This funny animal carries its own armor — a shell made of strips of hard material called *scutes*. When I got close to the armadillo, it rolled up into a ball. It was protecting itself because it didn't know I was friendly.

Your Friend

What you do:

1. Cut out the armadillo's head, tail, and legs from the first paper plate.

2. Cut out a ½" x 2" (1 x 5 cm) strip of cardboard. Bend the cardboard into a triangle, pinch the ends together, and tape to hold for a "stamp."

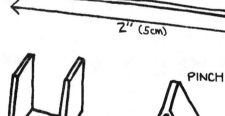

½"
(1 CM)

2" (5cm)

CUT HEAD, TAIL AND LEGS
FROM PAPER PLATE

PINCH

CONTINUED...

3. Dab the flat end of the stamp into the paint. Press it onto the second paper plate, and the head, tail, and legs for the armadillo's plates. Let the paint dry.

4. Fold the plate in half. Tape the armadillo's head, tail, and legs inside the plate. Tape the plate together. Use the marker to draw the eyes and mouth.

Site:
Uruguay and other parts of South and Central America and in Texas, southern Oklahoma, Louisiana, Arkansas, Mississippi, and parts of Florida

TAPE TOGETHER

AROUND the WORLD FUN!

⚙ **Animals with Armor!** Can you name other animals that have a protective outer covering like the armadillo? How about a porcupine? Now, you think of another one!

⚙ **Learn More!** To find out more about the armadillo, read *The Astonishing Armadillo* by Dee Stuart.

Antarctica

Of all the continents, Antarctica is the farthest south, which might make you think it's very hot. But not this continent! Antarctica is one of the coldest places in the world. It's actually made up of many mountainous islands. Guess what holds all of those islands together? A whole lot of ice! Sometimes this ice breaks off and floats out to sea. That's what makes all of the icebergs you see in pictures of Antarctica.

Believe it or not, tourists visit Antarctica, but there are no shops or schools. The only people living there are scientists who study the earth to find ways for us to take better care of it. If you ever go, better bring lots of mittens and scarves — along with your ice skates!

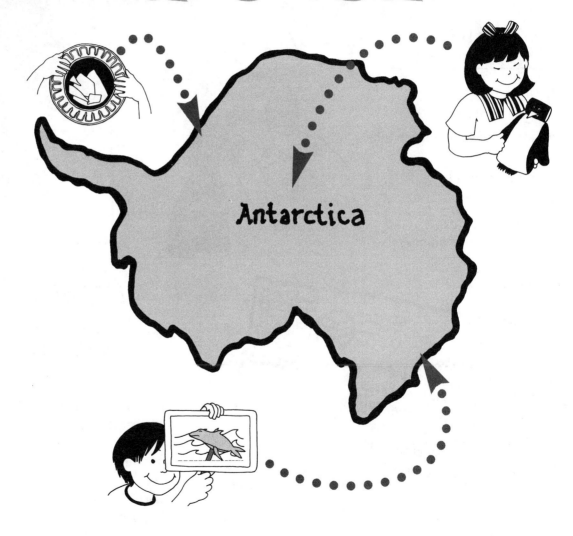

Adélie Penguin

What you need:

- White tissue paper
- Child safety scissors
- Cardboard toilet-paper tube
- Black tempera paint, in a dish or lid
- Paintbrush
- Construction paper (black and a scrap of orange)
- Tacky glue
- Wiggly eyes

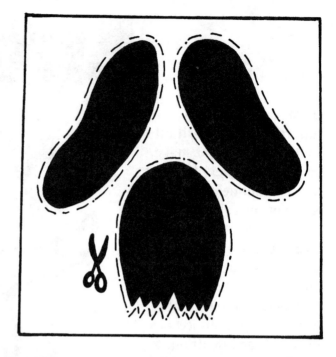

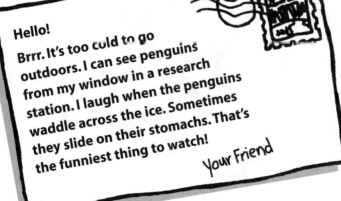

Hello!

Brrr. It's too cold to go outdoors. I can see penguins from my window in a research station. I laugh when the penguins waddle across the ice. Sometimes they slide on their stomachs. That's the funniest thing to watch!

Your Friend

What you do:

1. Cut out several layers of tissue paper longer than the cardboard tube. Wrap the tube in tissue paper and tuck in the ends.

2. Use paint to color the back of the penguin black. Let it dry.

3. Cut a strip of black paper and roll it into a tube for the penguin's head. Tape the end to secure. Glue on an orange paper beak and wiggly eyes. Then, glue the penguin's head onto the tube.

4. Cut out the wings and feet from the black paper. Glue them onto the penguin as shown.

AROUND the WORLD FUN!

⚙ **Indoor Snowflakes.** Do you know how cold it is in Antarctica? If you spilled a cup of hot water, it would turn to ice before it hit the ground! Make a snowflake that won't melt — out of paper! Trace a plate onto a sheet of white paper and cut it out. Fold the paper circle in half. Fold each corner into the center for a cone. Cut out shapes along the edges of the cone. Unfold the paper to see your snowflake.

⚙ **Funny Penguins!** Check out this website to learn more about penguins: **http://home.capu.net/~kwelch/penguins/**

Site:
Found on islands in the subantarctic and on cool coasts of Africa, Australia, New Zealand, and South America. Only the Adélie penguin and the emperor penguin reach Antarctica itself.

Icebergs

What you need:

- 2 Styrofoam plates
- Child safety scissors
- Clear or blue plastic wrap
- Transparent tape
- Blue construction paper
- Tacky glue

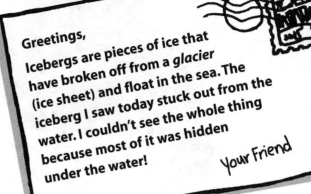

Greetings,

Icebergs are pieces of ice that have broken off from a *glacier* (ice sheet) and float in the sea. The iceberg I saw today stuck out from the water. I couldn't see the whole thing because most of it was hidden under the water!

Your Friend

What you do:

1. Cut out the center of one Styrofoam plate. Tape plastic wrap across the opening. Cut the center of the plate into iceberg shapes.

2. Glue blue paper onto the center of the second plate. Glue the icebergs onto the blue paper.

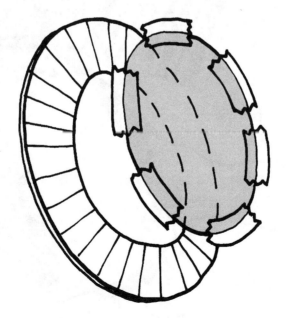
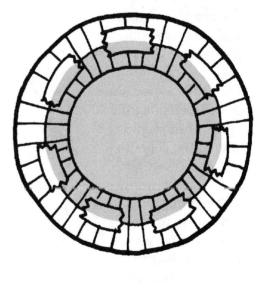

Site:
Common in both the Arctic and Antarctic regions and are often carried into lower latitudes by sea currents, particularly in the North Atlantic Ocean

3. Place the first plate upside down on top of the second plate. Tape the plates together.

AROUND the WORLD FUN!

⚙ **Silly Science.** Pour some water into a glass and add a couple of ice cubes. Now poke them down with your finger. They pop up again! The ice is lighter than the water, so it floats. That's what keeps icebergs from sinking to the bottom of the ocean!

⚙ **Disappearing Act.** Fill a container with snow. Let the snow melt; then, look to see how much water is left. Is the water level lower than the level of the snow? Snow takes up more space because it contains a lot of air!

Blue Whale

Greetings!

Before I leave Antarctica, I really want to see a blue whale, which visits polar waters in the summer. In the winter it moves toward the equator — the great imaginary circle around the earth's middle. The blue whale is one of the largest living things in the world; only a few trees are bigger!

Your Friend

What you do:

1. Cut out the whale from the blue construction paper. Glue the whale onto the stick. Use the black marker to draw on the whale's fins, eyes, and mouth. Use the blue marker to color the stick.

2. Glue construction paper onto the bottom of the tray for water. Cut a slit in the bottom of the tray.

3. Use the black marker to draw waves. Insert the stick into the slit to move the whale.

What you need:

- Blue construction paper
- Child safety scissors
- Popsicle stick
- White craft glue
- Blue and black markers
- Styrofoam tray (from fruits or vegetables only)

AROUND the WORLD FUN!

⚙ **Penguin Playmates.**
Another animal that lives in Antarctica is the southern elephant seal. Make elephant seals resting on an iceberg! Cut out four seal shapes. Take two and glue them together with a toothpick in between. Now, do the same thing with the other two pieces. Then, stick the toothpicks in an upside-down Styrofoam plate.

⚙ **Learn More!** To learn more about blue whales, read *Big, Blue Whale* by Nicola Davies and Nick Maland.

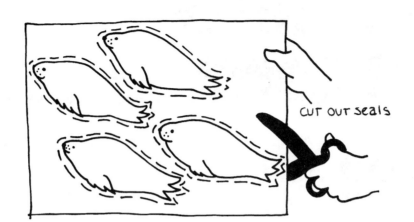

CUT OUT seals

Site:
Found in polar waters during the summer; moves toward the equator in winter

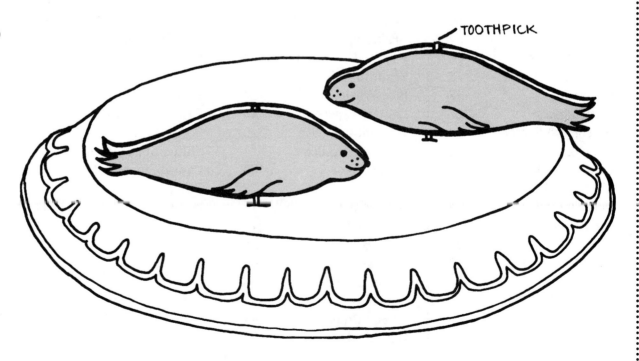

TOOTHPICK

Activity Index by Skill Level

Check the symbol at the beginning of each activity to quickly assess the challenge level.

Easy
(for even the littlest hands)

Medium
(requires a few more steps)

Challenging
(more involved projects)

More Good Books from Williamson Publishing

Williamson books are available from your favorite bookseller or directly from Williamson Publishing. Please see last page for ordering information or our website. Thank you.

More Williamson Books by Judy Press!

Over 500,000 sold!
Real Life Award
Children's Book-of-the-Month Club Main Selection
The Little Hands ART BOOK
Exploring Arts & Crafts with 2- to 6-Year-Olds

Parents' Choice Approved
The Little Hands BIG FUN CRAFT BOOK
Creative Fun for 2- to 6-Year-Olds

ARTSTARTS For Little Hands!
Fun Discoveries for 3- to 7-Year-Olds

Parent's Guide Children's Media Award
ALPHABET ART
With A to Z Animal Art & Fingerplays

Early Childhood News Directors' Choice Award
Real Life Award
VROOM! VROOM!
Making 'dozers, 'copters, trucks & more

THE KIDS' NATURAL HISTORY BOOK!
Making Dinos, Fossils, Mammoths & More!

 Williamson's *Little Hands*® Books ...
The following *Little Hands*® books for ages 2 to 7 are each 128 to 144 pages, fully illustrated, trade paper, 10 x 8, $12.95 US.

Little Hands PAPER PLATE CRAFTS
Creative Art Fun for 3- to 7-Year Olds
by Laura Check

WOW! I'M READING!
Fun Activities to Make Reading Happen
by Jill Frankel Hauser

The Little Hands PLAYTIME! BOOK
50 Activities to Encourage Sharing
by Regina Curtis

Early Childhood News Directors' Choice Award
Parents' Choice Approved
2000 American Institute of Physics Science Writing Award
SCIENCE PLAY!
Beginning Discoveries for 2- to 6-Year-Olds
by Jill Frankel Hauser

American Bookseller Pick of the Lists
RAINY DAY PLAY!
Explore, Create, Discover, Pretend
by Nancy Fusco Castaldo

Parents' Choice Gold Award
Children's Book-of-the-Month Club Selection
FUN WITH MY 5 SENSES
Activities to Build Learning Readiness
by Sarah A. Williamson

Early Childhood News Directors' Choice Award
Parents' Choice Approved
SHAPES, SIZES & MORE SURPRISES!
A Little Hands Early Learning Book
by Mary Tomczyk

Parents' Choice Approved
The Little Hands NATURE BOOK
Earth, Sky, Critters & More
by Nancy Fusco Castaldo

MATH PLAY!
80 Ways to Count & Learn
by Diane McGowan & Mark Schrooten

 Williamson's *Tales Alive!*® Books ...
These beautiful, full-color books focus on retellings of multicultural folktales accompanied by original paintings and activities. Books are 96 to 128 pages, full color, 8 1/2 x 11, $12.95 US.

Parents' Choice Honor Award
Benjamin Franklin Best Juvenile Fiction
Skipping Stones Multicultural Honor Award
TALES ALIVE!
Ten Multicultural Folktales with Activities
by Susan Milord

Teachers' Choice Award
Benjamin Franklin Best Juvenile Fiction
Benjamin Franklin Best Multicultural Book Award
TALES OF THE SHIMMERING SKY
Ten Global Folktales with Activities
by Susan Milord

Storytelling World Honor Award
BIRD TALES
from Near and Far
by Susan Milord

Williamson's *Kids Can!*® Multicultural Books ...

The following *Kids Can!*® books for ages 6 to 12 are each 144 pages, fully illustrated, trade paper, 11 x 8 $^1/_2$, $12.95 US.

HANDS AROUND THE WORLD
365 Creative Ways to Build Cultural Awareness & Global Respect
by Susan Milord

Parents' Choice Gold Award
American Bookseller Pick of the Lists
Oppenheim Toy Portfolio Best Book Award
THE KIDS' MULTICULTURAL ART BOOK
Art & Craft Experiences from Around the World
by Alexandra M. Terzian

Benjamin Franklin Best Multicultural Book Award
Parents' Choice Approved
Skipping Stones Multicultural Honor Award
THE KIDS' MULTICULTURAL COOKBOOK
Food & Fun Around the World
by Deanna F. Cook

TO ORDER BOOKS:

You'll find Williamson books wherever high-quality children's books are sold, or order directly from Williamson Publishing. We accept Visa and MasterCard *(please include the number and expiration date).*

Toll-free phone orders with credit cards:
1-800-234-8791

Or, send a check with your order to:
Williamson Publishing Company
P.O. Box 185
Charlotte, Vermont 05445

Please add **$3.20** for postage for one book plus **50 cents** for each additional book. Satisfaction is guaranteed or full refund without questions or quibbles.

Prices may be slightly higher when purchased in Canada.